David Alfieri & Uwe Sander

THE BASICS

OF POOL BILLIARDS

Begin playing the sport of pool billiards using the teaching methods of the THE POOL SCHOOL

www.billiardbook.com • www.litho-verlag.de

Print: Chroma Druck und Verlags GmbH
1. Edition 2005
Translation: Skip Newberry
Printed in Germany

ISBN 3 - 9804706 -4-4

This first book is dedicated to

Jerry Briesath.

Probably the worlds best professional pool trainer.

Content

Forward

When you think about it, pool is a pretty weird sport. No other sport is quite like it. During play, there is no reaction from your opponent when you hit the ball as there is in tennis or forced moves as in chess. There is no body contact like in boxing and even if one said that golf were its closest relative, they are in fact worlds apart. Golfers have their own personal balls and every golfer is responsible for his or her lay. In pool, my rough lay can suddenly be your problem. A golfer concentrates and reacts to his individual situations on a playing field, against all opponents at once and is always allowed to mark a scoring card. In Pool, you may loose and never have had a chance to shoot a ball.

Maybe one or more of these examples, is the reason why the pool sport has become so popular during the last 2 decades, here in Germany. Flicks like "the Hustler", "the color of money"; "Baltimore bullet" or "kiss shot" and others have certainly helped its popularity as well. However, the youngest discipline in pool, "9-ball" has pushed aside 8-ball the more traditional game here in Germany, with its colorful variety of rules. In doing so, 9-ball has created a fast and easy chance for Beginners to check out what is really happening behind the scenes. If one takes this one step further, one begins to realize the broad spectrum of participants. Men and women, senior's and children, beginner and professional tournaments and/or club leagues, where all of them are trying to figure out daily, how to move the balls the best way possible on the green felt. How old one is doesn't matter, which of course is a positive factor for its popularity. Most professionals start playing at an early age, around 6 to 8 years of age. However many pro's have started much later. The question, at what age should I retire, is neither answerable nor relevant. Those of you who have fun at this game will always be ready for a match. World champion 3 cushion player and pool billiard legend Willie Hoppe, (1887-1959) won his first world title when he was 18 and his last 47 years later, at the age of 65! We can assure you that even after winning his last world title he was still having fun at the game. How young or old you are and how good or lesser good your game tends to be – if your having fun at it and you want to get better, then this first book will certainly help you get where you want to go.

Acknowledgments

The work invested on this was and is an experience, which for us, has not only been rewarding but a lot of fun as well. We've learned how very unique this sport is, when one has the goal to write about this sport in all of its details, and to our readers in such a way, that the beginner or free-time player as well as advanced players profit from it. Without the help from friends, club members, players and employees, this effort would have been extremely difficult. If we were to name every one of them, then it would take up too much room. So we have decided to name only the most important, to which without them the making and publishing of this book would not have been worthy.

Our biggest thanks goes to **Jerry Briesath**, founder of the Pool School USA, who helped and supported us in the making of the Pool School Germany in Europe. He was an indirect factor for the first book (in German) and he personally edited the translated version. He is honored for having initiated the foundation, through his American teaching concept, the way we administrate and manage the Pool School Germany in Europe and for his wise and important tips (not only in pool) and his incredible, to which he was always happy to give.

Because of this, we learned the two most important factors a trainer needs to know how to do before he can teach. 1. The art of being able to prove the reasoning behind a statement before making it. 2. The art of being able to relate this fifty different ways.

Thank you, Jerry.

We never got a chance to meet **Jack H. Koehler**. We got a hold of his book during our trip to Chicago in 1993, getting this document was a very important objective of ours. We bought it in the same Pool hall where Paul Newman and Jacky Gleason filmed "The Hustler". It was autographed by him, was the very last copy and belonged to the owner of the establishment. The owner, while watching us devour the pages with interest, began to realize what an impression this book was making on us and sold it to us immediately. Our thanks goes to Jack H. Koehler for waking in us the creativity we needed, how to relate pool in different manners and for giving us the permission to use a portion of his work. We hope, one day, to meet and get to know him personally.

Writing and publishing a book requires a great amount of cooperation between the writers and the publishers. Getting any book into print on this subject matter, especially when it's being translated into another language, is no less important and very difficult. We want also to thank Thomas Lindemann and the LITHO-Publishers for his patients and support. Since this is not the first book Thomas Lindemann has had published, we are certain our book is in the good hands of an experienced publisher.

There are so many more who have motivated and helped us create this first volume, to refer to them all would mean to name the better part of our students and friends. In this way, we want to thank all of you who helped and supported us along our way and be complemented by the fact that the first volume has finally been accomplished.

Frankenthal, autumn 1997, 2005

David Alfieri, Uwe Sander.

This books goal

The goal of this book is to explain, just like in any other sport, there are two elements a player needs, to move to the next higher level of competition: **Knowledge** and **ability**. Or as Jack H. Koehler through the use of two relevant questions had put it:

1. "Do I really know (knowledge), exactly where to hit the ball, to make it go into the pocket?

And

2. "Am I physically able (ability), to hit it there?

There is however, one other point to remember when using these two elements and that is through your method of approach. Knowledge alone may not be enough to raise ones ability. However, through your "method of approach" you can declare a fast, effective and sensible means for developing your ability, from any knowledge obtained. Used correctly, this will always show an obvious and prompt orientation for your games success.

The better half of all beginners in pool and even some of those who have been playing the game for while, are confronted with a problem eventually, information management. Everybody wants to help you and your getting flooded with information from all sides. Are you familiar with this? Somebody relates to you a "show and tell" example on how to do a "real" draw shot and another explains it to you exactly the opposite. Whether you are trying to develop a straight delivery or a good stroke, the best stance, or find out what the deal is with the "stop-ball". You always have friends and good players around, who "know the answer". Whether their answer is right, wrong, or just misleading is secondary. The fact is, almost everyone will try to pass it on to you and though it was the same question, you are still lightly confused.

As a beginner, what are you supposed to do – even those who have been playing awhile? What is useful, what is not? Is there a system to this madness on how to separate the good from the bad or misleading information? What are my options?

If you take these ideas and try them all out on your own, you are going to lose a lot of precious time (decades!), until you find the best ones. However, what if we can show you a real system to this problem? Namely this system has been able to separate the effective from ineffective over the past two to three decades. In addition, what if, this system can also explain why something is effective and another is not?

Be this as it may, there is one thing for certain that you are doing right! Research! This is the correct manner for understanding similar problems. Answers to these questions is the reason for this first volume and the reason why this book be rendered the most important book in our series. We hope that after reading this first edition, in the future you will be able to set apart the answers to your question as either effective or ineffective.

Introduction

Uwe Sander and David Alfieri
(Licensed trainers under the Billiard Congress of America)

Before you begin with the readings, we would like to introduce a few important matters and terminology.

The biggest part of this book goes on to explain the knowledge we, in the past 10 years, have obtained and to which is being delivered in our courses in the Pool School Germany. To possess knowledge and the ability is one thing, but to pass this knowledge on, so that anyone can understand it, requires just as much time and talent. We learned this immediately at a seminar in Bad Hennef, Germany, where Jerry Briesath gave a lecture in 1989. He would explain in 20 minutes subject matter and get everybody to understand, where other trainers would need hours or days. He would explain it to you in a variety of ways, through situations out of every day life or through other types of sport, until you got the message.

During the years 1991 and 1992, we traveled to Madison, Wisconsin and attended the American Pool billiard Academy (Pool School USA) of Jerry Briesath to qualify as licensed *BCA-trainers. Upon our completion of this course, we invited him to the opening of the Pool School Germany, in Germany, where he held courses. This in turn offered the opportunity to studying his training techniques more closely.

Between 1992 and 1997 around 600 students, private and from billiard clubs, from Germany and around Europe, have attended courses held at the Pool School Germany and enjoyed a refreshing new way to learn a beloved subject matter. Most of these students come back for refresher or advanced courses. Some come to attend our (strenuous) instructor's course so they can teach their own students. A greater part of our students had asked whether our teaching methods were in a book one could acquire. Therefore, after answering enough intelligent questions with stupid answers, we decided to write the book you are now holding.

It was of course clear to us from the beginning that after becoming certified BCA Instructors; our work would not be left to, "just instructing". Research for the improvement of learning methods was our goal. During the past few years, we have gathered numerous books, videos, reports and learning concepts, interviews and conversations with other trainers and players. Many were tested for their sensibility or nonsense, whether they were systematic or unorganized and how the mortal needs of the student could be met. Whether it be a technical and tactical or a physical and mental aspect, we looked into it. Those books, which were important, made sense and contained a greater part of our expectations and learning concepts have been listed later in this book under "reference material". We have organized and systemized our teaching concepts through this research and we intend to extend our goals by introducing an instructor's handbook, so that our methods and concepts taught at the Pool School Germany can aid them, when they teach their own students.

While technique the basic learning point is in all billiard areas, we decided to write more volumes about this, rather than only one basic book. Such a book of course would be complete, however it would not allow us to go into detail.

In this book, we use descriptions such as ***Beginner*** or ***Novice***, Hobby or Amusement players, League or advanced players, Pro-Am, semi or full Professional players. The Beginner is described as being an absolute stranger to this game/sport and has seldom held a cue in their hands, whereas the Novice is at least "wet behind the ears". They both may have gathered a little "theoretical knowledge" along the way. However, the similarities in both types of player are the lack of practice. Both types of players miss easy balls regularly and have no real feel for the game.

Hobby or ***Amusement players*** have been playing longer and even though they enjoy this sport regularly. They only play for fun and are satisfied with their level of play and for the moment are not really interested in gathering more knowledge about technique or theories toward the betterment of their game and always seem to make the same mistakes.

We categorize ***League players*** as Amateurs as well as Advanced, semi-Pros or even Professionals as well. The greater part of these players to which is being referred here, belong to the lower leagues and though they have much practice at their game, many of them haven't quite grasped the connection between theory and practice, which they may have (incomplete) received through their league trainer or maybe a better player. League players (because most participate in open and league tournaments) are always interested in bettering their game.

The ***Advanced player*** (may be described also as a pro-Amateur or semi-Pro) has a good grasp for the connection between theory and practice. They invest a good part of their free time in the study and betterment of their game. These players continue to improve physically as well as mentally.

The ***Pro-Am*** or ***professional*** is the last level that a player reaches. However, when you get right down to it, their level of play is similar to that of a top advanced player with of course two important differences.

1. The Pro – as a rule – plays high-level competition more often.
2. They are sponsored by companies who have trust in their ability.

The class descriptions we have listed above are, of course symbolic and should by no means be a strict classification for everybody playing this sport. Consider these classifications as flowing. They help us relate to the reader, different perspectives and relations for better understanding.

We also wish to advise the reader to work with these readings chapter for chapter, as they build upon each other. Further, terminology that will be explained in depth in later volumes, a fact that we can't seem to get around always, will sometimes be touched on in this book too early and unless defined outright during the passage you can certainly find it in the glossary.

Throughout this book as well as in later volumes, we attempt to describe everyone who plays pool as players. As non-gender, meaning men as well as women, boys and girls, left-hander as well as right-hander. Further, with ambidextrous players the training diagrams expand for use with both hands. No need getting too one-sided during these exercises, right? As for now, enjoy yourself and let us begin with the successful development of your game.

1 Playing accessories

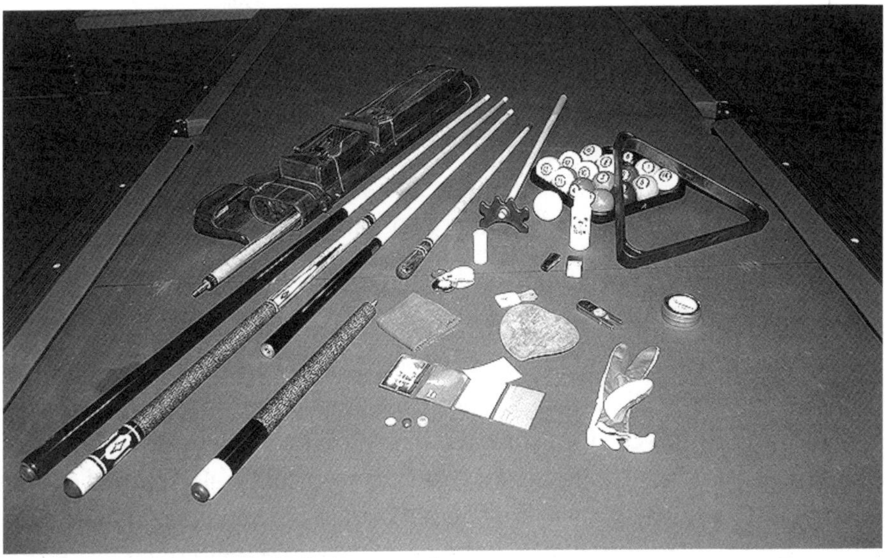

Diagram 1: Pool billiard playing accessories

Just like in any other sport, pool billiards has it own array of accessories, of which all players who are interested in this sport, should be acquainted with. This chapter does not confine this to a mere listing, but goes on to explain in depth, background information, which is not only helpful but interesting as well. Much of this information is certainly strange to the beginner or hobby player, however could be of much help later for their – hopefully – upcoming successful career.

1.1 The Cue

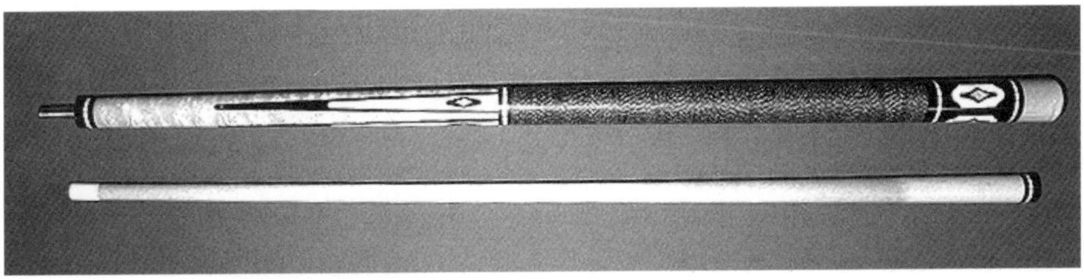

Diagram 2: Two-piece cue

Playing Accessoires

Probably the most important tool for a player is the cue. Usually it is the first piece of equipment a player acquires after becoming serious at getting better at this sport.

The player can acquire cues that can be broken down in two, three and more parts. House cues, found in establishments for the public, are usually of the "one-piece" version. Most amateur to pro cues, break down in two pieces; the upper (shaft) bridge half and lower (butt) grip half of the cue. Many cue makers produce the grip half or butt out of three pieces (see chapter 1.1.7 production).

Because they are glued together, we refer to them as one piece.

Although so called "Break" or "Jump" cues can break down in the grip half through a "quick-out" joint even further, Jump cues are still referred to as two-piece cues. Cues, which can be broken down in three or more pieces, are more compact for easier transportation. They are of course compact; however lack the handling and quality of serious cue makers to which serious players rely on. Because of this, we will concentrate our interest primarily on two-piece cues.

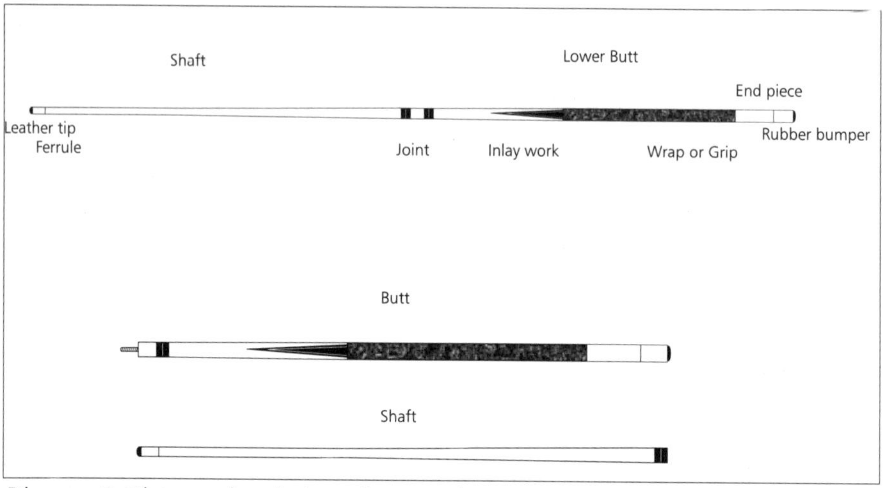

Diagram 3: Element description of a two-piece cue.

The cue is the primary tool a player requires to move the cue ball into an object ball and serve that into a given pocket. The simple idea that it's nothing more than a wooden stick, used to apply speed and direction to the cue ball is rather naive (gimme a broomstick for this and I'll sweep the

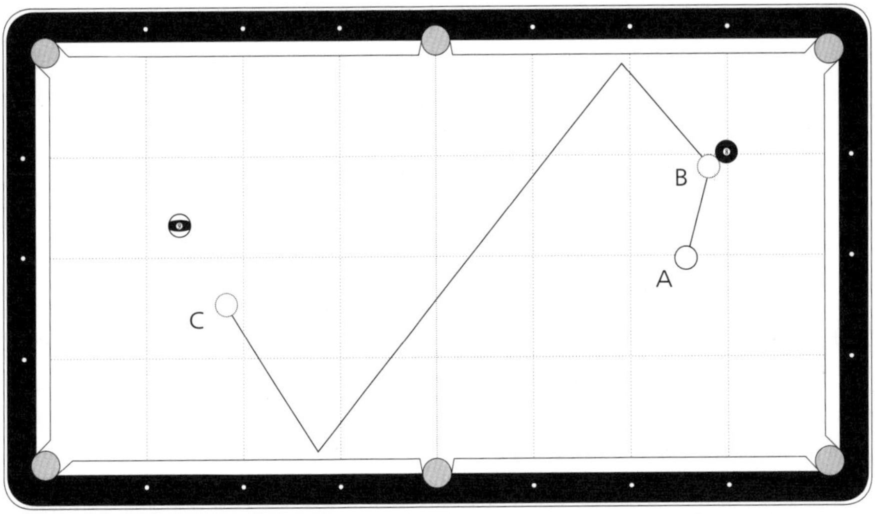

Diagram 4: The cue is the primary tool a player requires to move the cue ball into an object ball and serve that into a given pocket.

place up after winning this tournament!) but theoretically possible... One should realize that today's cues from their beginning, have been constantly refined and modernized to make play more accurate. Hardly... that a top pro would attempt to compete at a masters tournament with any old cheap house cue he may have found, and then go on to beat everybody, is hardly thinkable.

The beginner or novice should start with a price worthy, quality, brand named, cue. Shy away from cheaply made house cues which tend to warp, have cue tips that are either flat or practically nonexistent or are screwed on, have scratched or damaged ferrules or all these characteristics. If this sport should be more than just a past time, you should consider investing in your own personal cue. Not only pros, "most players" rely on their own personal cue. A sound reason behind such a decision (next to its high quality) is its familiarity. You can become accustomed to it, rather than always having to adapt to different weights, tip or balance characteristics of the cues available to you in public pool halls.

Now the beginner, at this point, may be unfamiliar to the importance these characteristics have toward the rapid development of their game. They are however, of the utmost importance in regards to reliable play. This is covered thoroughly in this chapter.

Brand new, good quality cues are as low as $100. However, before buying, you should try a few out first. A rule of thumb: How does it feel in your hand? Where is its balance point (weight distribution)? Is it top heavy or butt heavy? The length and the weight of the cue are of great importance and something one always should consider before buying.

1.1.1. Cue length

Providing you are of normal height between sixty-six and seventy-two inches, then a cue should measure between 57.5 and 58.5 inches. Normal production length is around 58 to 58.5 inches to which smaller people can normally adapt. However, for optimized play, your cue should adapt to you and not otherwise.

Cues which need to be more than 58.5 inches can be ordered extra through most manufacturers, however be careful at this point. Given a standard length of 58 inches and lengthening the shaft to 59 inches is not a problem, (if you have an extra shaft, send it in as well). If you wish to lengthen your cue anything over an inch and a half, then you should send the entire cue in to be lengthened. The lengthening should then be evenly distributed to the shaft as well as the butt portion of the cue otherwise the characteristics of your shaft, its elasticity as well as to the cues overall balance begins to become impaired the longer the shaft gets at this point. Alongside of that, a longer shaft that lengthens your cue to 59.5 or 60 inches may not fit in your cue case anymore.

Smaller people as well as children should play with cues depicting their height. If a cue is too long, then the weight distribution becomes impaired. The butt hand tends to grasp the cue on or around the balancing point. For example, a child using a cue of standard length with an open bridge will find it harder after a follow through stroke, to keep the cue tip from rising up off the bridge hand. Whereas, a cue tailored to their height, will keep the butt hand well behind the balance point, where it needs to be.

1.1.2. The cue weight

In the beginning, most players get used to a cue, which looks good, plays good and to which the weight plays, for the time being, only a secondary roll. The weight of a cue however does make an impression toward its handling and playing characteristics and should always be considered before making a final decision. Through the following examples, at least during shots with a soft stroke your cue should not be heavier than what you are physically able to control and be comfortable with.

The weight of a cue, in its extremes, is normally between 16 and 23 ounces (oz.). Metric system would equal 450 and 600 grams (gr.). Amateurs to Pros play with cues weighing between 19 and 21 oz., whereas most of them have narrowed this down between 19 and 20 oz. You can usually vary the weight by doing one or more of the following steps:

- Changing the weight screw: The smaller or lighter the screw, the lighter the cue.
- Lengthening: The longer the shaft of course the heavier.
- Type of joint: The heavier the material, the heavier the cue.
- Through inlay work: Depending on the material used a cue can be made heavier or lighter.

By doing one or more of the above, will of course not only change the weight of the cue, it will also redistribute the balance point as well, to which will be gone into further detail in a later chapter. The weight of your cue will affect the amount of dynamic rotation you apply to the cue ball as well as the distance covered when rendering identical stroke techniques. Try out cues weighing between 16 oz. and 21 oz., and see which weight feels better for you, keeping in mind that most professionals use a cue weighing between 18.5 and 20 ounces.

In order to create movement to the cue ball (legally), a certain kind of force is required, namely "kinetic energy", which is initiated by spearing the point of the cue against the surface or face of the cue ball. The distance a cue ball covers has a lot to do with the weight and speed generated against it from the cue. Through the use of a lighter cue, one would need to spear (stroke) the cue faster through the cue ball than would be needed when using a heavier cue to reach identical kinetic reactions.

Through the sum of this fact, one can better understand the following rules when deciding between the lighter or heavier cue.

The lighter the cue, the harder it is to stroke straight through, when hitting hard.

On the other hand, with the use of a lighter cue, situations where precise positioning is required and the distances are much less, one can develop a better feel for the cue balls speed.

Therefore the lighter your cue, the better your speed control, however the lesser your exactness may be when a powerful stroke is used.

The amount of spin applied to the cue ball is to a small degree due to the cue weight, especially when the stroke energy is high. Because a heavier cue will move easier through the cue ball, than a lighter cue does, its forward movement is therefore less hindered and more fluid, which allows the cue to keep its speed through the cue ball.

Consequently:

The heavier the cue, the more spin will be applied to the cue ball, when struck horizontally outside of its center (English).

Should you find this useful, then let us look at this as positive. On the other hand, if one wishes to apply spin to the cue ball, while stroking the cue through it from a vertical angle (massé), thereby miscuing… then the results may be quite negative to the cloth, to the leather tip or both when using a heavy cue.

The novice or beginner is well advised to start out with a cue weighing 19 oz., as they will find it easier to develop a straighter and smoother stroke. After a while, when the players technique becomes stronger, they can move up to the weight of 19 or 19.5 ounces in order to develop their speed control even more. If however, one still tends to have problems developing their technique, it may be wiser to move the weight up to 21 oz. However, the beginner should always keep these two points in mind.

1. A change of cue, in the beginning, is always different, but usually brings forth advantages.

2. Eventually one needs to decide on a cue that feels comfortable.

The weight of a cue holds two other things to which the characteristics of its playability are affected.

- The balance point:
- The weight distribution:

1.1.2.1 *The balance point*

The balancing point is that point, which when balancing horizontally, where the cue is at its heaviest. It should be between three quarters to an inch and a half from the front of the grip wrapping.

The position the balance point may have, can be further influenced by:

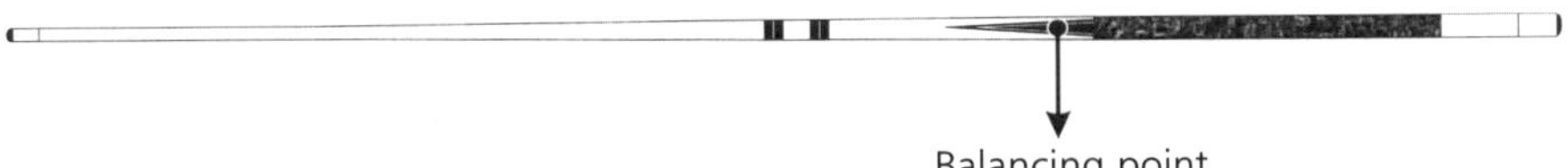

Diagram 5: The balancing point on the cue

- The length
- The entire weight
- The joint between the upper shaft and butt (plastic, wood or metal) and
- The weight screw located in the butt of the cue.

The position the balance point has, determines whether the cue has more or less weight lying on the bridge hand, (top heavy or butt heavy).

A cue with its balance point further to the rear, for example a 23 oz. cue with a plastic joint, bears for the smaller player or child the problem with uncontrollable movements during the follow through as well as dur-

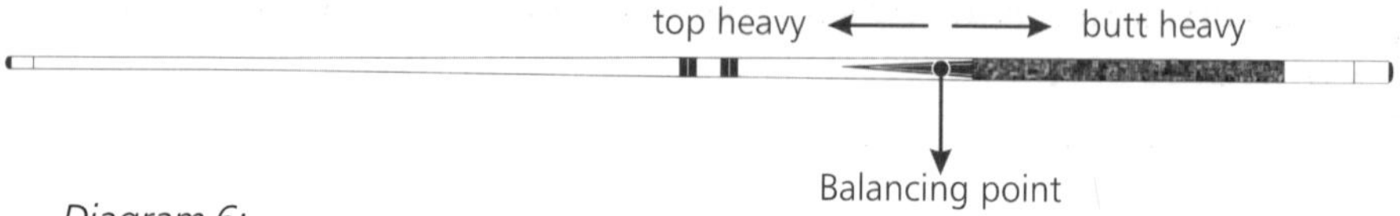

Diagram 6:

ing warm-up strokes, as they tend to grip the cue on or close behind the balancepoint.

Such players require a cue where the balance point is closer to the joint, than the grip.

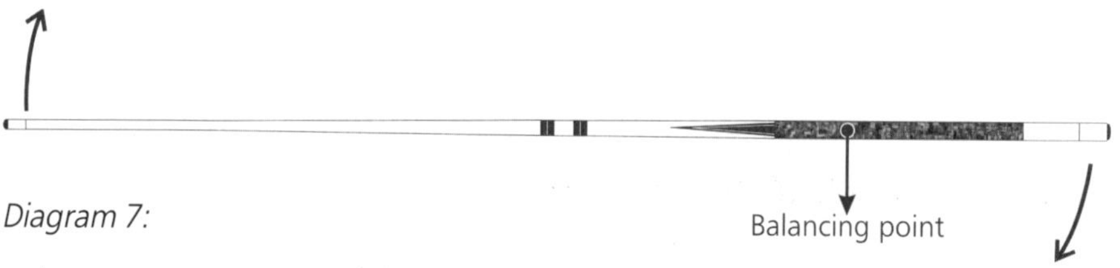

Diagram 7:

1.1.2.2 The weight distribution

The balance point is influenced through weight distribution. Weight distribution is also primarily responsible for the reliability conveyed to the fundamental nature of a given device. For example: A dart, a feather ball, an arrow or a spear all have their weight distribution directed to the middle or front of its body so that it will fly and stick (as in a dart, or a spear) or land on (as in a feather ball) a surface properly. While the cue is not considered a throwing device (although a few, manic distressed, brazen and sometimes inebriated chaps, have tried to prove otherwise), the weight distribution as it were, is unavoidable. If the cue were designed more similar to a

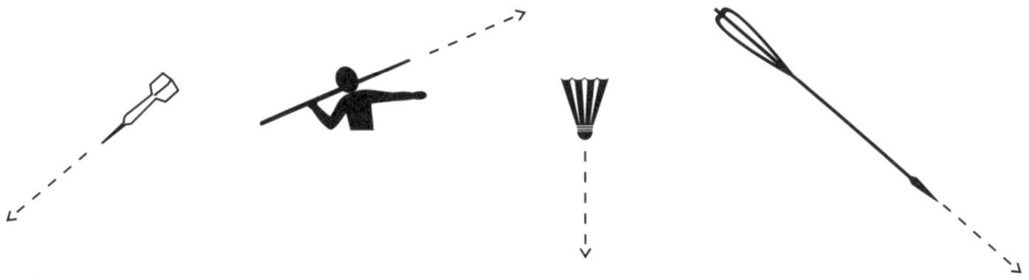

Diagram 8: Weight distribution in equipment of other sports

spear, where the balancing point finds itself more to its middle, then the laws of physics would consider it a sound body. However, because the cue form is of a conical nature, the bulk of its weight is directed toward the end of the cue and is therefore considered an instable body.

Due to the cues normal unstableness, the player needs to use both hands to convey its fundamental nature effectively. This means, poking balls with both hands on the cue, exactly towards desired directions, consistently.

1.1.3 The cue tip

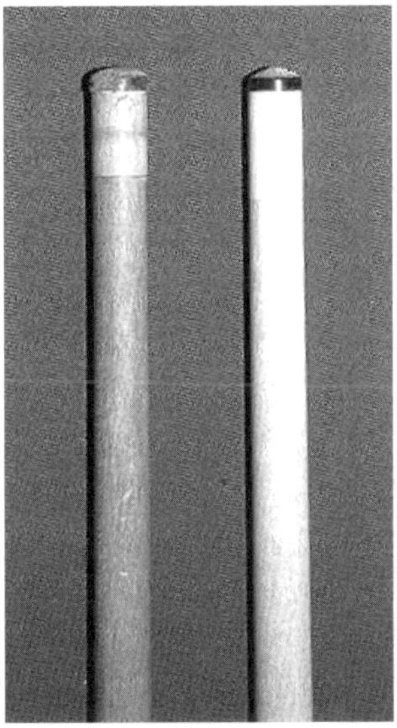

The leather tip has been in public use since 1823. It is said that a Frenchman demonstrated its use in America. The American and British observers at that time were quite astonished in the width the action radius had been greatened, through its use without miscuing. True, other materials have been tested since then, however due to their inconsistency, no other has matched the wide spread acceptability during normal play that leather has enjoyed. Most tips are made of ordinary rawhide. Leather is very durable and the best material against miscuing and deformity as it normally regains its

Diagram 9: old and new

original form quickly after contacting the cue ball. (This diagram shows an exaggerated example.)

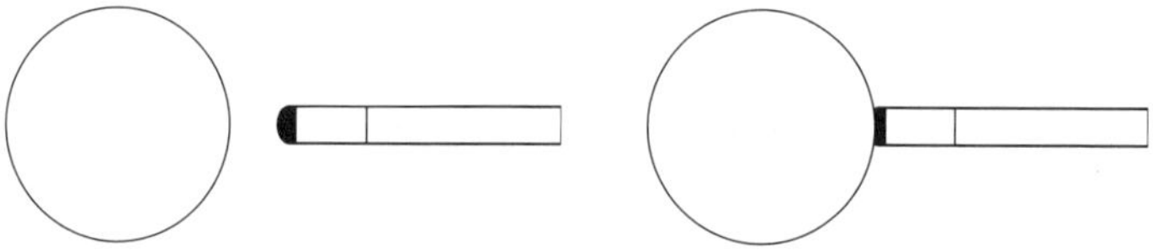

Diagram 10: Cue tip behaviour

During this contact, which is similar to a shock absorber, a high amount of abrasion is created. The use of chalk, which when applied to the tip, magnifies the abrasion effect extremely and allows the player to apply an infinite amount of spin to the cue ball (English or masse), which is sometimes important for moving the cue ball in or to its next ideal objective or shape area.

1.1.3.1 The leather density

How hard or soft a leather cue tip is, plays an important factor to its playing characteristic. One can test the hardness the cue tip has by simply pressing the edge of your thumbnail into the face of it. Of course the deeper the impression, the softer the tip is.

Hard leather tips cannot be dented with the thumbnail easily. Other than knowing if a tip is hard or soft, has left research in this area, open for discussion as to which type is better or worse. Fact is, the production of harder tips is much more expensive. The inexpensive, softer tips also have a slight drawback. They will eventually begin to deform (mushrooming), and become harder anyway. Under extreme circumstances (For example: A massive miscue to a poorly chalked, mushroomed cue tip), bits of leather can be torn off.

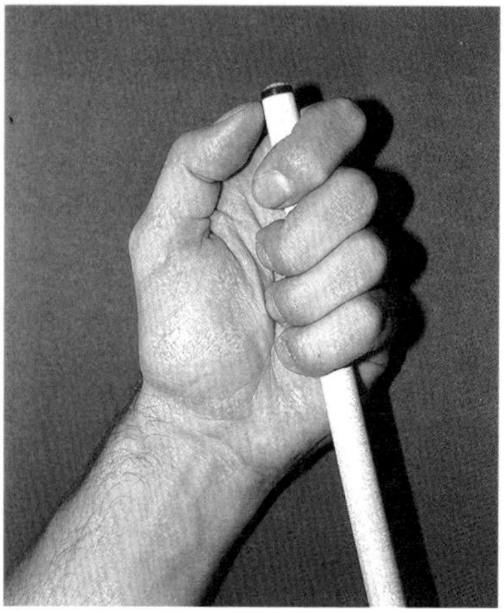

Diagram 11: The hardness a cue tip has can be checked by pressing the thumbnail against it.

The disadvantages of a soft cue tip:

- Soft tips loose their desired form rapidly and can become flat.
- Soft tips absorb shock better, however one is often motivated to hit harder.
- If no attention is given to its reforming, it eventually becomes hard anyway.
- Because of frequent reforming, the life-span is short.

The advantages of a soft cue tip:

- Soft tips create a greater touching surface when striking and thereby reduces the risk of miscuing when applying extreme outside English to the Cue ball itself.
- Soft tips absorb chalk much better.

Although these advantages seem encouraging, the advanced player on up will rather play with a harder cue tip. Its form and playing characteristics remain longer. The use of a softer cue tip will loose its form rapidly after hitting the cue ball. In time, it begins to mushroom off the sides and the center of the cue tip becomes hard as well. If no attention is given to it regularly, then it is best to change the cue tip entirely. This „hardening effect" will happen faster, when the same cue is used for the break as well. It is therefore a wise decision to invest, acquire, or borrow another cue for this job.

1.1.3.2 Types of tips

A professionally groomed cue tip looks as shown in diagram 12. If the cue tip is hard and flat, it will miscue, if the cue ball is struck with it, further outside of its center. The reason for this is that the cue tips surface needs to resemble that of the cue balls round surface, otherwise the

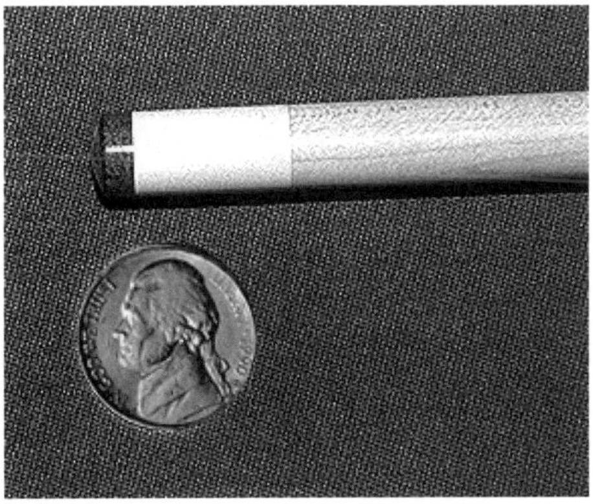

Diagram 12:

abrasion applied, will be only a fraction of what it needs to be. The strong exaggeration shown here below may help for better understanding.

The following tools are used to form and groom the cue tip:

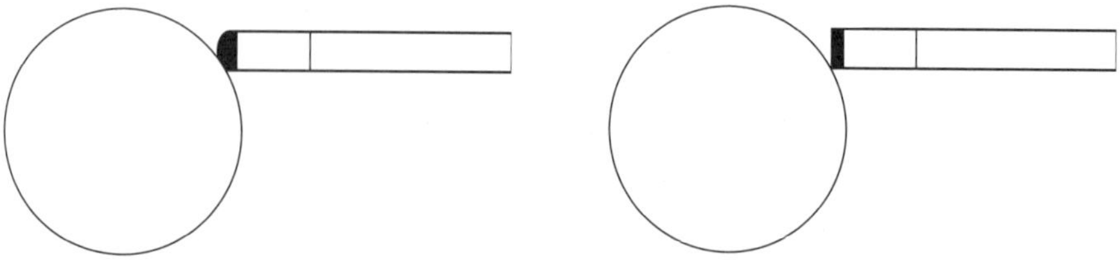

Diagram 13: Rounded cue tips touch a greater area on the cue ball, than flat cue tips. (Excerpts from: The science of pocket billiards, from Jack H. Koehler)

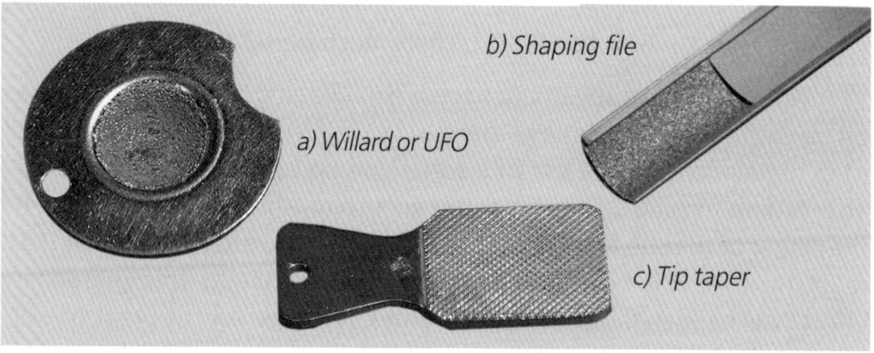

Diagram 14: Tools for the leather tip

a) this tool is used to shape the curvature of the cue tip. Here the importance lies in shaping the tip surface evenly (as shown above). b) This tool is used to sand off any overhangs to which a softer tip tends to build on its side. Be careful not to scratch the ferrule. c) This tool roughens the surface of the tip so chalk can be easily accepted.

There are types of tips that screw into the ferrules and there are those in which are glued on. The advantage of a screwed-on tip is that when damaged or worn out, it can easily be replaced. This advantage however, is found mainly in cheaper cues, where the handling characteristics are a far cry from quality. Locations, where this sport is taken more seriously, their managers will dig a little deeper in their pockets and supply the player with quality house cues. These only have tips that are glued on. Though requiring a little more maintenance, they are much more durable and can usually meet the wishes of the hobby and free-time player. You will rarely find an amateur and probably never catch a pro playing with anything other than cues of the glue-on variety. There is a good reason for this. In order to create a cue with great hitting characteristics, many factors need to be considered during its construction. We will dwell a little deeper here.

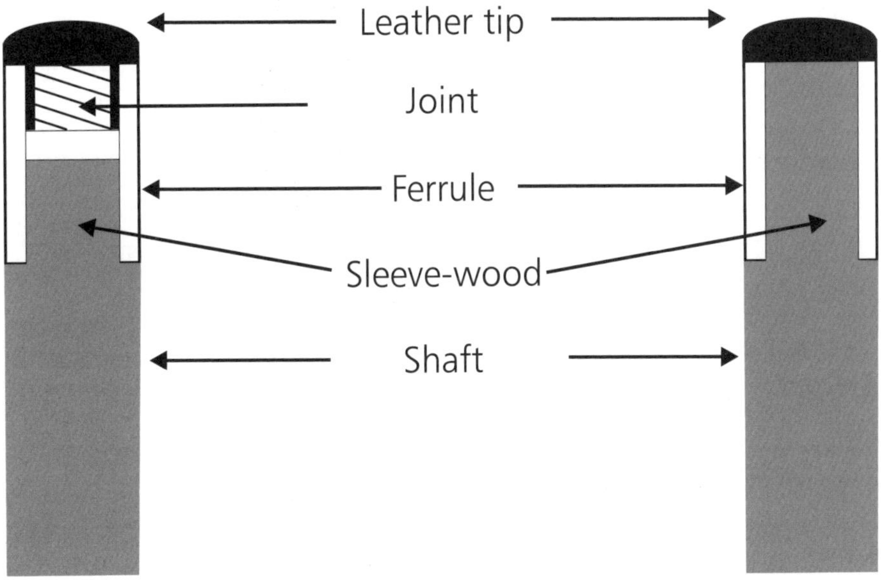

Diagram 15: Screw-on vs. glued-on leather tips

Among these factors is its "air tightness". No play should ever be allowed between the leather tip and the ferrule! If the force transfer from the cue to the ball is not 100 percent solid, you will certainly have good reason to be disappointed with the entire cue. Screwed-on tips do not always have this 100 percent "air tightness". Further, a glued-on tip transfers the hit to the shaft over the ferrule better, whereas screwed-on tips apply most of the impact directly to the ferrule and may damage it prematurely.

Furthermore, let qualified personnel re-tip your cue properly. This does not cost all that much and a good reason for buying a two-piece cue with an extra shaft. Professional advice and maintenance for the cue's long life and eventual resale value should be of some concern to its owner. Its sound characteristics and performance is given a chance to speak for itself.

1.1.4 Ferrule

The ferrule is a round cylindrical (usually white or cream colored) plastic or plastic fibered protector located behind the leather tip and sleeved evenly onto the wooden shaft.

Diagram 16: Ferrule sleeve

1.1.4.1 Composition

Ferrules formerly would always be made of ivory, buffalo horn or similar materials. Today's ferrules are mostly made up of a durable (sometimes fiber supported) plastic composition, which have similar characteristics. Some house cues have metal ferrules, to which may be sturdier, however can bear the danger of damaging the cloth. Further, metal has a higher vibration coefficient, which under extreme conditions, may even be damaging to the wooden shaft.

1.1.4.2 Purpose

Its purpose is the dispersion of shock the leather tip has received and spread it evenly to the wooden shaft. This helps against premature damage. (As seen in diagram 15, a good example how this energy dispersion works). Along with this, it has another important purpose as well. The ferrule is a good aiming aid, either when aiming on the cue ball where you need to hit it or as „helper" with warm-up strokes, to see if you are stroking the cue in a straight line. This and other methods for controlling your warm-up strokes will be handled in detail, in a later chapter.

1.1.4.3 Types of ferrules

- The standard ferrule
- The ferrule for screw-on tips

As seen in diagram 15: the principle construction in both types of ferrules. The standard ferrule supports the shaft end and the base of the leather tip, which is the reference standard design for dissipating the shock between the cue ball and shaft. The ferrule for screw-on tips, as shown, does not work together with the shaft and receives the greater portion of shock energy. Damage can be rendered prematurely, to the ferrule itself or the shaft. For this reason, screw-on ferrules are mainly used with cheaper cues.

1.1.4.4 Care and treatment

Ferrules need, not like cue tip leathers, no great care or maintenance. However, one should avoid miscuing or shoveling under the cue ball, which under extreme circumstances can eventually damage the ferrule. Keep the ferrule free of chalk, as these markings can distract your aiming concentration but really shows everyone how you take care of things.

1.1.5 The shaft

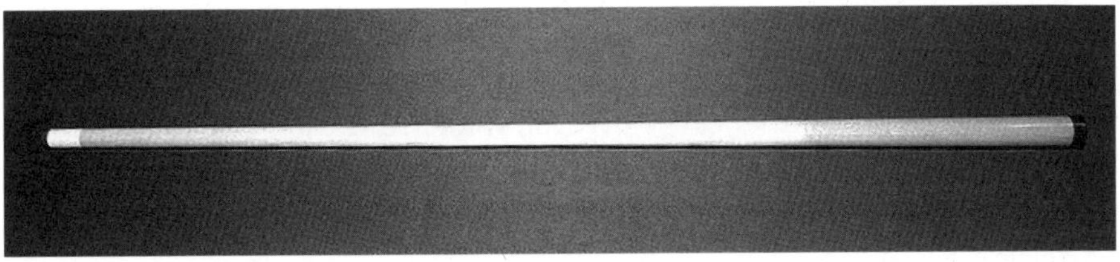

Diagram 17: Shaft portion of the cue.

The shaft including the leather tip and the ferrule is the heart of every cue. The cue can be cheaply or expensively made, however if your shaft has a problem with it, then your game (as well as your enjoyment) will have a problem with it as well.

1.1.5.1 The shaft constitution and construction

Good shafts are made mostly out of hard wood maple. Shafts for cues of the cheaper variety are made out of long leafed pine. It is quite a bit softer than maple, can warp easily and is not as expensive a material as maple. A good shaft is straight and lightly grained. If the graining of the shaft is strong, uneven or has knots in it, then it is very likely to warp. Such

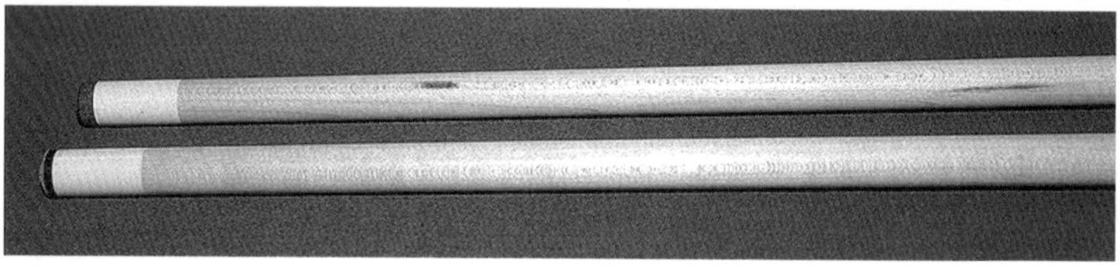

Diagram 18: Shafts with and without visible signs of graining.

a shaft can also draw your attention away, while aiming. The more inconspicuous your shaft looks, the better. A brand new high quality shaft is practically white in appearance.

High quality shafts are turned on a lathe in steps, over a great period to build up its warp resistance. During each step, a thin portion is shaved off. By doing this, which needs several months to stabilize, the inner tension of the wood is relaxed in grades and thereby helps the wood retain its new form easier. Each step strengthens its final form. The chance that a quality shaft will warp is thereby greatly reduced. Cheaper shafts are turned on a lathe, in a single process. The chance that it will warp, is somewhere around 50:50.

Before buying either one however, make sure that the shaft is absolutely straight. Any deviations will only get worse as time goes on, regardless of the quality. However, with quality products, there is always the chance of getting a new one.

Standard diameters for shafts range from 12 to 13.5 mm., this applies for the ferrules as well. How stiff or flexible a shaft is depends on a number of factors.

- The shafts overall length.
- The shaft diameter.
- The shaft form (conical form or a professional taper).
- The type of wood used (hard or softer sort). The Craftsmanship (simple or extensive lathe work).

Flexibility and sturdiness play a major roll toward a shaft's good playing characteristics and this, of course, begins on how it was constructed. The player must determine how much elasticity a shaft should have, by testing out a few. Be careful while testing here however, as prolonged use of this or that shaft distorts a biased opinion. A good rule of thumb is; first impressions are lasting, which in this case means, if you can make balls with a particular shaft from the beginning, you will get along with it later as well, so test another immediately.

1.1.5.2 Measurements

The length and diameter a shaft has makes a difference in the overall balance of the cue. The thicker and/or longer the shaft, the further towards the joint the balancing point will be relocated. Many players use shafts with a diameter between 12 to 13 mm and around 28 to 29.5 inches long. Beginners are well advised, to choose a shaft similar to these measurements.

1.1.5.3 The taper

There are two types of taper. Conical and Professional taper. A shaft with a Conical taper gradually grows in width from the ferrule to the joint. Cues with a professional taper however, have the same diameter as the ferrule for roughly 12 to 14 inches before the conical form begins to grow again to the joint. Both forms have their advantages as well as disadvantages, which become relatively meaningless when a decision has been reached.

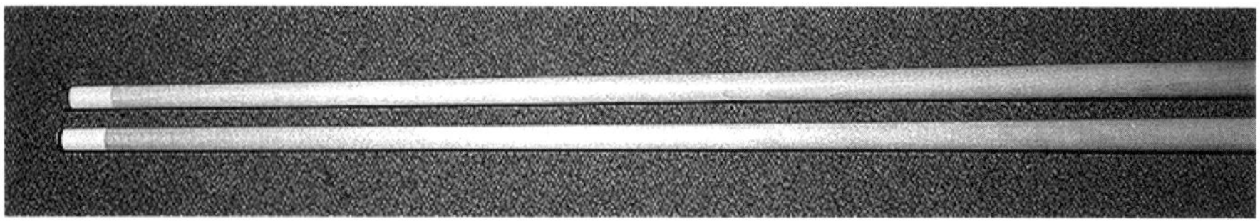

Diagram 19: Parallel or professional tapered (below) and conical shaped (above) shafts.

The conical formed shaft presents the problem for the "closed bridge" as the diameter of the shaft is continually increasing or decreasing and is therefore difficult, in the beginning, to retain complete comfort and control. Further, during the follow-through, one tends to hit a higher point on the cue ball than originally intended, because of the shafts ever increasing thickness. The biggest, while singular advantage a conical shaft has is its directing quality. When applying extreme sidespin to the cue ball, for example with extreme left English, the cue ball will initially move to the right, known as the "Squirt" phenomenon.

Conical formed cues stay straighter during such a hit than do cue shafts with a professional taper, thereby reducing this phenomenon considerably.

Cue shafts with a professional taper allows the bridge hand to form itself around the stroking rang much more comfortably and completely. A correctly formed closed bridge reduces miscuing considerably as well. However, the Squirt is much greater.

1.1.5.4 Care and treatment

Many players occasionally use rough to very fine sandpaper to remove the chalk-dust, talcum powder, and other filth films, which gradually form in time on the shaft. This method however, if used too often, will reduce the cue shaft diameter considerably. If one, while using only fine sandpaper and sanding very lightly, does this, 1000 times they would loose 1 millimeter in the diameter of the shaft. This can be felt, because the ferrule diameter remains the same. This in turn, will increase in time, the characteristic "squirt", or deflection in the shaft of which you constantly adjust to. After losing 2 to 3 mm of diameter and replace the shaft with a new one, it becomes apparent because you cannot seem to adjust or just can't make "those shots" you normally made with the old shaft. Therefore, use this method sparingly and refrain from changing the shaft characteristics at all. A shaft, lightly sanded once, before or after a tournament, will hold its original form closely for about two to three years.

There are other treatments for the care of your cue which cost a little more time and may not be designed to render shortly before a tournament, they are however better when considering high quality resale value and no change to the shafts playing characteristics. Consider the following: Wring a wet cloth until it is damp and does not drip. Apply an amount of either a normal bar of soap or dishwashing fluid. This allows you to clean your shaft thoroughly, however be careful not to soap up the leather tip, especially if it's a hard leather. The properties of the soap such as lanolin, etc. may expand and soften your leather, if it's allowed to be soak in. Afterwards, rinse the shaft thoroughly with a clean damp cloth until all soap film has been removed. Then immediately dry the shaft with a towel. Air-drying the shaft with a hand held hair dryer afterwards as long as it is not too hot insures that all moisture has evaporated.

1.1.6 The joint

The joint is that part of a two-piece cue which joins together the "upper shaft" to the "lower butt". It can be made out of wood, metal or plastic. The material from which it is made plays a relative roll in the overall playing characteristic of the cue itself.

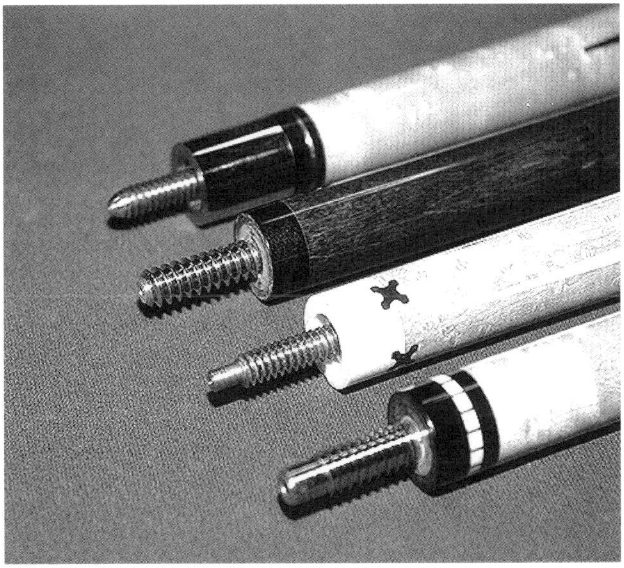

Diagram 20: Various types of joints.

- The heavier the material, the more the balancing point moves toward the joint, which therefore increases the weight to the bridge hand.
- The lighter the material, the more flexible, and deflective the shaft is.

1.1.7 The butt

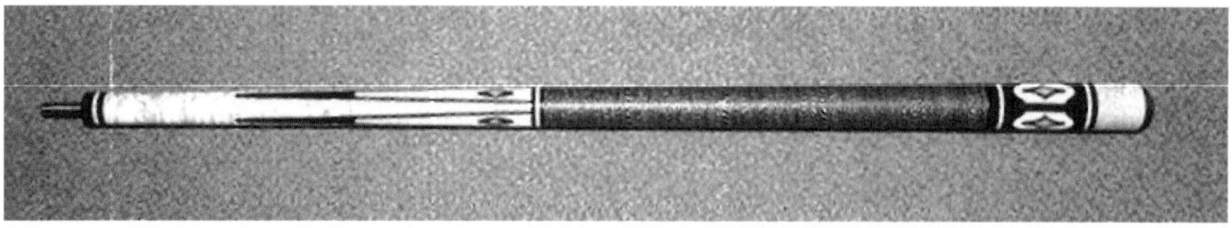

Diagram 21: Butt portion of a professional cue.

The butt can be made out of a variety of woods. Contrary to popular belief, the butt is not always made of a single piece of wood but rather two, sometimes three different types of wood and more. The major portions usually are first intricately formed or "crowned", then are glued and fitted together perfectly for extra stability. (See chapter 1.1)

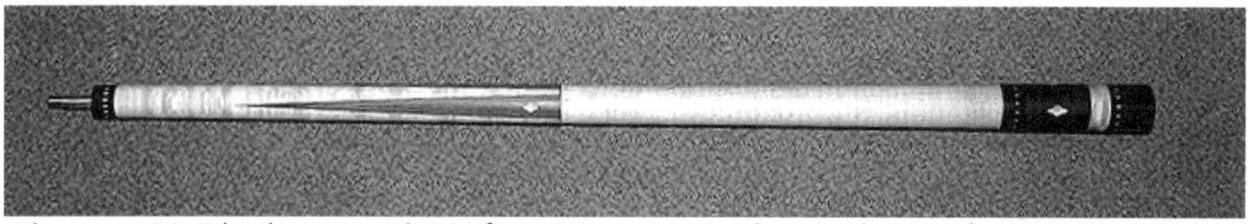

Diagram 22: The butt portion of a cue appears to be made up of a singular piece of wood...

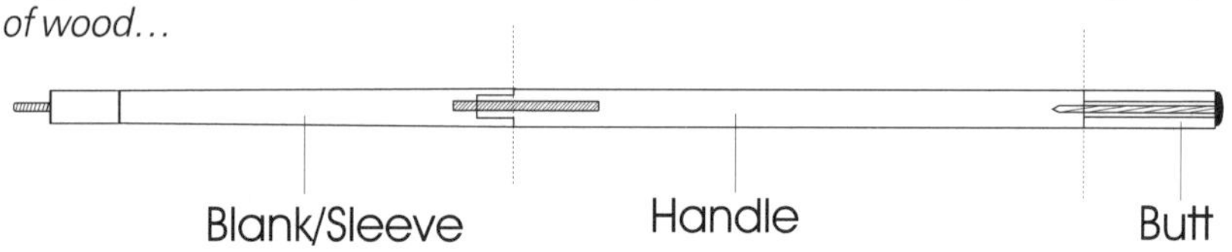

Diagram 23: ...but in reality is made up of three individual pieces.

Although the design of the cue, i.e. color, inlay work, type of wood, manufacturer, etc., plays an important roll in most cue purchasing decisions, the wrap handle of the butt should play the most important.

It can be made of leather, nylon, Irish linen, rubber, or even the plain varnished that protects the wood. The point here is, when playing, your hand should easily glide along the grip as well as easily brake when light grip tension is applied. Either the grip should feel slightly abrasive or your grip hand should not be prone to sweating. For example: If when playing with a cue whose grip is of plain-varnish wood and nervousness cause the palm of your hand to sweat, you'll have to grip the cue tighter than otherwise normal. This could have negative side effects during the warm-up strokes into the follow-through. Further, while trying to mentally relax the cue may slip out of your hand entirely! Considering this may help you decide on what is right for you.

1.1.8 The rubber end (Bumper)

The end of the butt should have a bumper made of rubber. This bumper is important for the butt end, as it may be fragile and/or very expensive and this portion of the cue is constantly meeting the floor that may or may not be carpeted. It also prevents slippage when leaning the cue against something and should be so designed that at whatever normal leaning angles you use, the actual butt of the cue never contacts the ground.

Diagram 24: Rubber bumper

1.1.9 Workmanship verses quality price

The workmanship between manufacturers varies greatly, and there is an immense number to choose from, of which the better half represents high quality. A very misleading and widespread opinion is; "The quality lies in the price". This is not entirely true. It is true for the most part that a cue, under $50, is of lesser quality than one, which exceeds $400. Nevertheless, if someone tried to prove that the playing characteristic of a cue costing $1000 is better than that of a good $400 cue, he is not being entirely truthful. In fact, there are good beginner models starting as low as $75 to $100, which for the beginner is even well recommended. Of course, if you want "mother of pearl" inlays or a fancy design from a brand named manufacturer, you will be over $500 very quickly.

When buying a new, quality cue, every part of the cue should be free of any flaw. Here are a few tips, aside from its alluring design, one should be aware of before purchasing.

- Shaft and butt should screw together noiselessly and easily.
- Shaft and butt joint should fit together perfectly, allowing no overhangs. This goes for leather tip to the ferrule to the shaft as well. Everything should join perfectly and smoothly together.
- Watch for stress fractures, which may only be detected during play. No clicking should be heard. It may only be that the leather is not correctly mounted. Listen for a satisfying "thud" when hitting the cue ball.
- Check the ferrule and butt end for cracks or scratches and other damage.
- The lacquered finish should be immaculate between the joint and wrap of the butt. No dents are discovered.
- The inlay work, if any, should be smooth and perfectly designed. No trace of glue under the lacquered finish can be seen.

Roll the shaft over a flat, clean, level surface and observe the distance between the shaft and surface closely. If it wavers more than an eighth of an inch or more than 2 mm, you should not consider buying it, then it is definitely warped and will only get worse. This test should be performed on the shaft only.

How a cue looks, from its extravagant design or intricate inlay work, does not influence the playing characteristics one bit. Whether the cue is brush painted in fluorescent yellow, has super hero comic figures, or has the classic style, what you buy is what you get. The design you choose should "turn you on". In effect, you are selling your personal style and signature to the sport. This in turn should mentally motivate you to play well and for most of us, it does. It can get to the point where a person yearns for that cue that is "one of a kind" in order to reinforce his personal individuality and strengthen his mental motivation. Since there is a lot more to learn mentally than physically in this particular sport it may now be easier to understand why one would pay such a high price for a particular cue.

1.1.10 Protective measures

When purchasing a cue or if you already possess one, a cue case should not be left out of the price. The cue case is indispensable during travel as it protects against temperature differences as well as other obvious dangers. For this reason it is recommended that a sturdy case be acquired. If you ordinarily leave such things in your car on a frosty or hot summer day, be sure that your cue case can withstand these extreme conditions for short periods of time. An automobile however, should not be

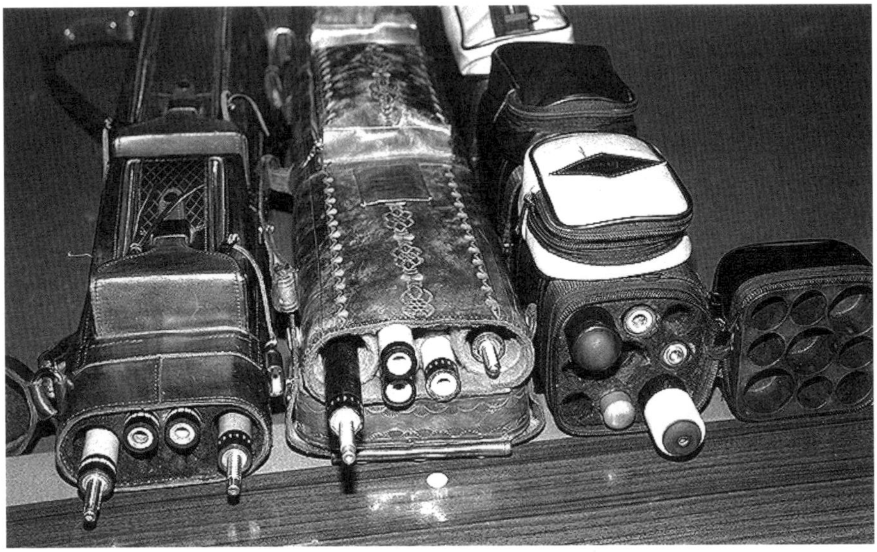

Diagram 25: Cue cases

considered a permanent storage area for any cue case. Your cue normally has at least two different materials to which the heat or sub zero temperatures reflect, metal and wood. The stronger influences the weaker and in this way, your cue will warp eventually.

Another protective measure would be, do not lend your cue out to just "anybody". Especially if they cannot afford your personal preferences, are not in your will and testament and do not highly respect you.

1.1.11 The break cue

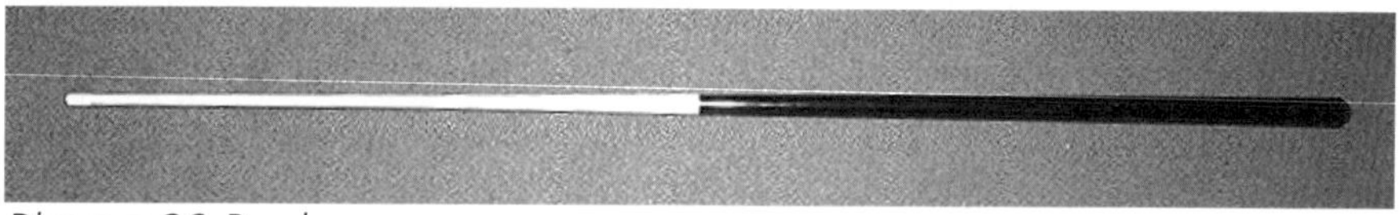

Diagram 26: Break cue

In Europe, during the last 5 to 10 years, the introduction of the break cue is becoming increasingly the rule, in which primarily the break of an "8" or 9-ball rack is always used. Almost all pros utilize a break cue of some sort. Most are simple with no extravagant design, just for breaking cue and prices range from $75 to $150. The reason is not primarily to hinder any warping to the main cue but rather the premature deformation to the cue leather or ferrule itself. Under these conditions, the main cue's tip will be exposed unnecessary to premature hardening, deformation or even tearing portions off it. If the tip is thin, the break can crack the ferrule as well, especially if a miscue is provoked.

The ideal weight of a break cue has yet to be measured definitely. However the preferred weight lies somewhere between 18 and 21 oz. The key lays in the technique, and then even pros are undecided whether the cue should be heavier, lighter, or just as heavy as the main cue and "technique" varies greatly in this sport. For this reason, we must ask you to experiment with these weights. Find out what is best for you.

1.1.12 Jump cues

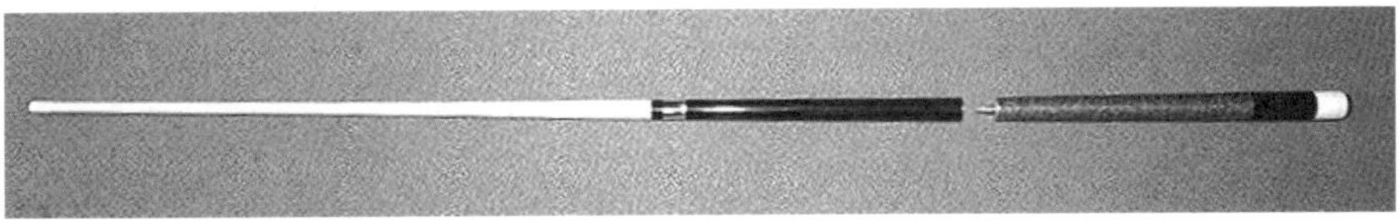

Diagram 27: Jump cue

Jump cues are used for special shots, to which the name has been given. Its design makes it easier to jump the cue ball over other balls, which are close and in the way of a straight-in or normally easy shot. When aiming with a jump cue into the cue ball, you are actually driving it, at the onset, directly into the plane of the table surface itself, not shoveling it. Driving the cue ball into and through the playing surface is of course impossible and in turn, the cue ball has no other way to go but "up"! Aiming at a slighter angle to the table surface, when the distance between cue and

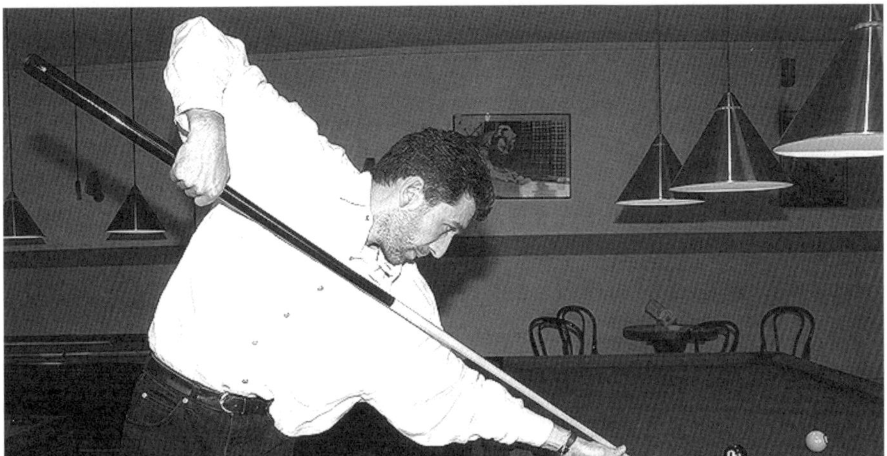

Diagram 28: Jump shot with a normal cue

object ball is further away from one another, the entire cue can be used to make the cue ball jump easier assignments. Because the method of delivery, especially for those of who are not as tall, is exceptionally different from normal play, the study of the jump ball began primarily with the shaft portion of the cue. Mainly, because the delivery was found to be easier to control and later that the weights of the shaft itself played a deciding roll, the steeper the jump angle is. The lighter the instrument used, the higher or steeper the ball can jump. These two methods (entire cue or broken-down shaft portion of the cue) for jumping over the cue ball were up until a few years ago, often observed in tournaments. It has only been during the past few years that the introduction of specially made cues, especially

Diagram 29: Jump shot with a broken down jump cue.

designed for this purpose been marketed, to include new rules for the minimum length a jump cue is allowed to be. These cues can be broken down to two thirds their normal size. The break cue has a second joint, which can be unscrewed often faster than the main joint.

If one were just beginning to learn this sport, buying at the onset such a break-jump cue would be overdoing it a bit. It would be wiser to experiment with your normal cue at slighter angles at first. Time and experience will help you decide later what is right for you, not to mention eventual bargains.

1.2 The table

There are a number of ways a good table can be identified and not solely because of its brand name. Qualified personnel should assemble the table, as the correct assembly an important prerequisite is toward ideal playing conditions. The table should be quite heavy, extremely level and the cloth, probably the players most important criteria, should be strongly spanned and of high quality.

Diagram 30: Pool table

1.2.1 Measurements

The playing field is double so long as it is wide. Its length will always identify the size a table has. For example: 7 foot, 8 foot or 9 foot. A 9-foot table is therefore four and one half feet wide and an 8-foot table is 4 feet wide and so on. If you use the metric system, you will need to convert this: 1 foot equals 28.2 cm. The playing field should be between two and a half to 3 feet high. Tables for tournament play are as a rule 9-foot tables, whereas 7-foot tables are commonly found in barrooms, because space is a rare commodity. They are usually coin-operated. 8 foot tables were designed for home use, however you need an area of at least 321 sq. feet and for a 9 foot table 331 sq. feet, where the width be not lesser than 16' 3.5". Although larger tables, for the beginner and amateur, require better aiming technique, the smaller tables require better position play as the crowding factor becomes more defined.

1.2.2 Training aid markings

During training, especially when training basic layout patterns and situations, i.e. aiming and/or stroke technique, the best method for remembering previous layouts is by marking them first with chalk. Although as will be mentioned later as one of the best ways to soil the table, these marking can be removed thoroughly with a damp cloth quickly. Allow these dampened areas to dry completely before continuing play.

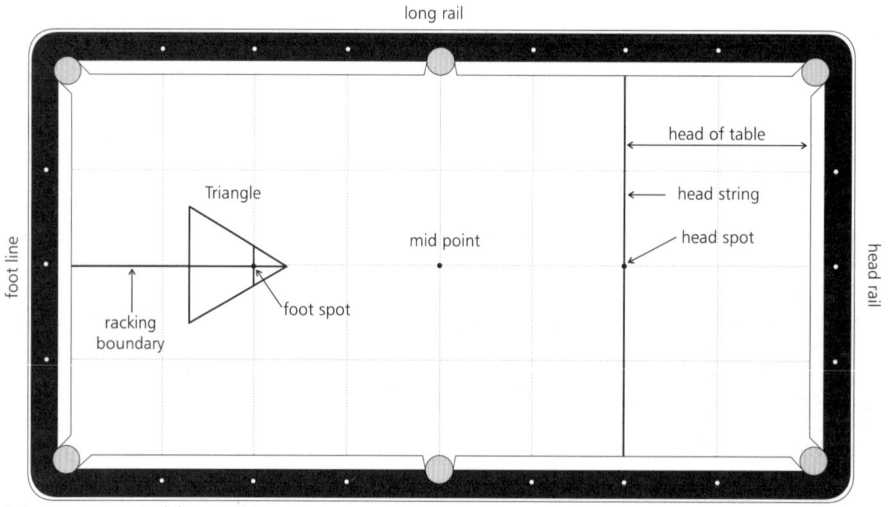

Diagram 31: Table markings

1.2.2.1 The method of marking the playing field

The method for marking a freshly laid playing cloth is as follows:

1. Start at the head-string, to create a feel for the marking instrument you are using. If you make a mistake here, it is not quite as bad as making one while outlining the triangle on the foot-string. Orient yourself with the second diamond on the side rail from the head of the table and using a yardstick or something similar, draw a line between these two diamonds

Diagram 32: Table markings at the head of the table

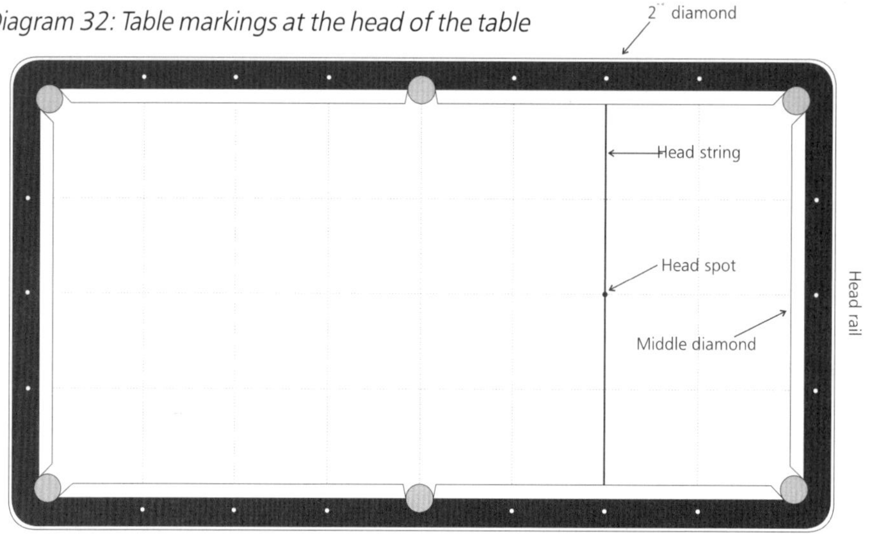

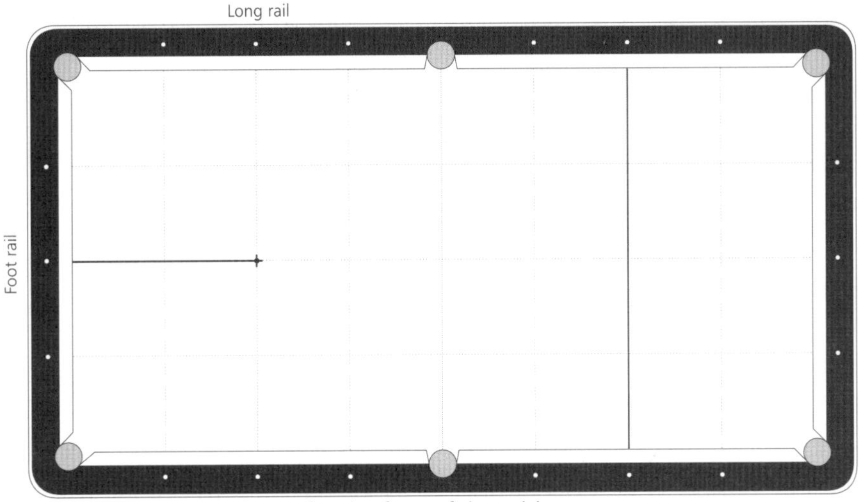

Diagram 33: Table markings for the foot of the table

across the entire width of the table. Mark a point in the middle of this line, which is on line with the middle diamond of the head rail. This is the head-spot.

2. With the help of diagram 31, determine where the foot spot is and mark this with a plus sign using a ruler or similar tool. The foot spot should be in line with the second diamond from the foot of the table's side rails and the middle diamond of the tables end rails. Draw a line from the bottom of this plus sign to the middle of the foot rails middle diamond. This is

Diagram 34: Using the table markings for game setup.

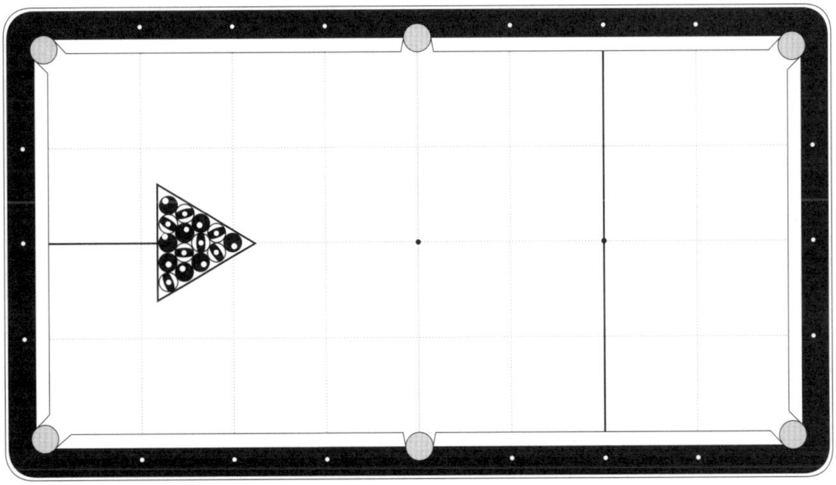

the foot-string.

3. Place a ball exactly on the foot spot and create an indentation there by knocking on the ball with another ball lightly. Done correctly, the ball you have placed on the foot spot will hold its position easily.

4. Carefully rack-up the remaining 14 balls with the help of the triangle up to and against the ball on the foot-spot. Making sure that the ball on the foot-spot does not loose its position. Check the middle ball, in the row of balls, closest to the foot rail and see to it that the foot-string divides this ball exactly in the middle. The racking triangle is now ready to be outlined with your marking instrument.

At this point, it may be wise to get the help of a second person. One to hold the racking triangle in position and the other to outline the rack perfectly. If you own or run your own pool hall and are marking a number of tables, be sure to mark each table with its assigned racking triangle. The racking triangle should be made of sturdy wood or plastic composition that does not easily bend. During the course of time the table markings may fade to the point where they may need to be retraced, this is of course optional.

1.2.3 The rails

These are the six individually mounted rubber cushion, which outline the playing field, and redirect a moving balls forward movement. The bumpers are covered with the same material as the table after being per-

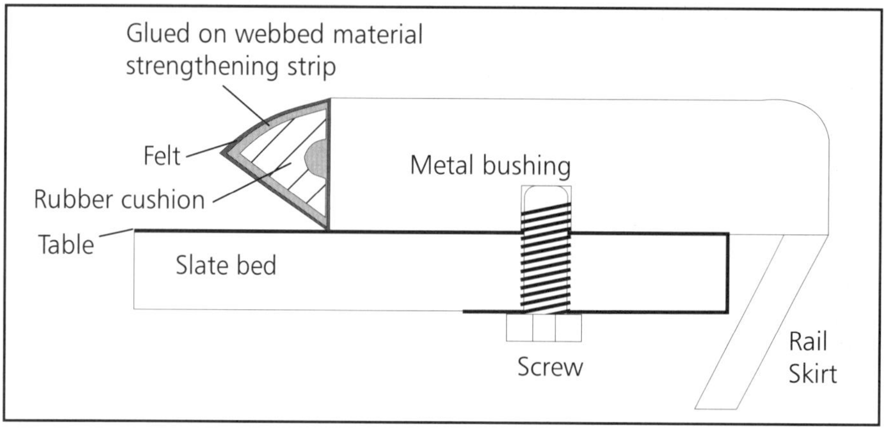

Diagram 35: Cut away view of the rail construction of a typical professional table.

fectly mounted with a highly professional industrial adhesive. The mounting of the rubber bumper to the rail is an exacting art. If the bumper is too high, the balls will travel to slow. If the bumper is mounted too low, the balls will bounce off the table. Therefore, the height of the bumper is very important and we are talking between one-eighth and one-sixteenth of an inch or 1 to 2 mm along the entire length of the bumper system! The rubber bumper must properly and completely adhere to the face of the rail. If not, the ball will be hitting what is known as a "dead rail". This will deflect the ball unconditionally in those directions you would not normally expect the ball to go. On the other hand, bumpers correctly mounted to the rails create a lively playing field. Balls bounce back livelier, than during their original approach. Pros love a table with these qualities because their "feel" or "touch" becomes a predominant factor and nerves play a deciding roll. Extremely well mounted rails can allow the cue ball to reach up to 9 rails successively, however the average table allows only 6 to 7, which also allows for good maneuverability as well.

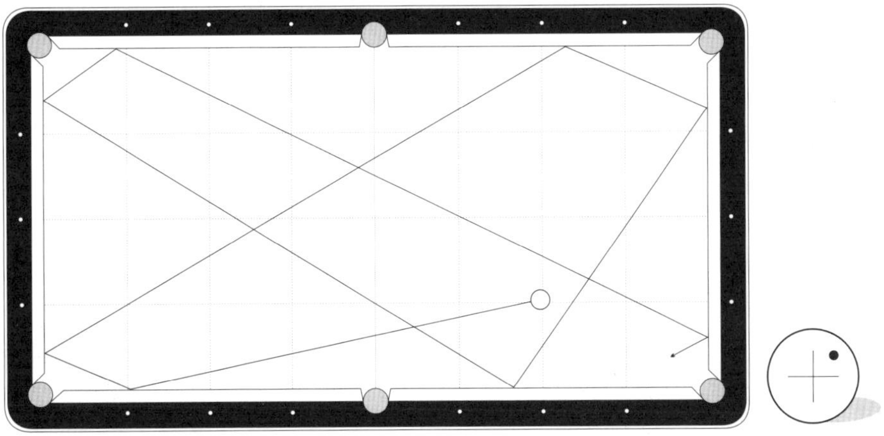

Diagram 36: Rail rebound test

Unless a table is weathered by the elements, such as wind, rain and sun, the only thing that needs to be replaced regularly is the cloth. Contrary to popular belief, the rubber bumpers very rarely need to be replaced, unless they (through extreme climate conditions) become rock hard and show signs of cracking. Remounting is much more likely required. It is therefore very important however to farm this job out to qualified, pool table specialist.

1.2.4 The pockets

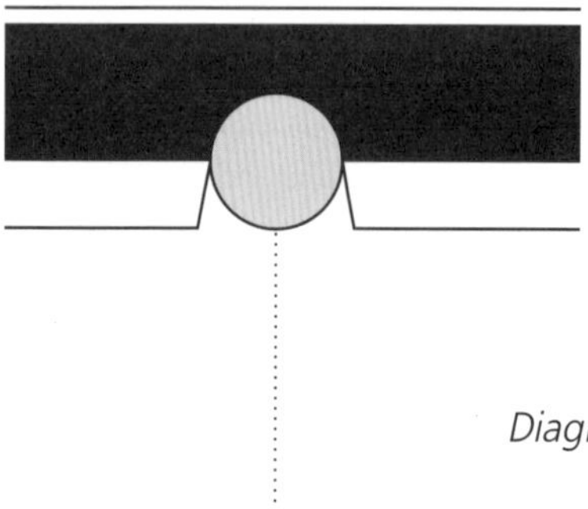

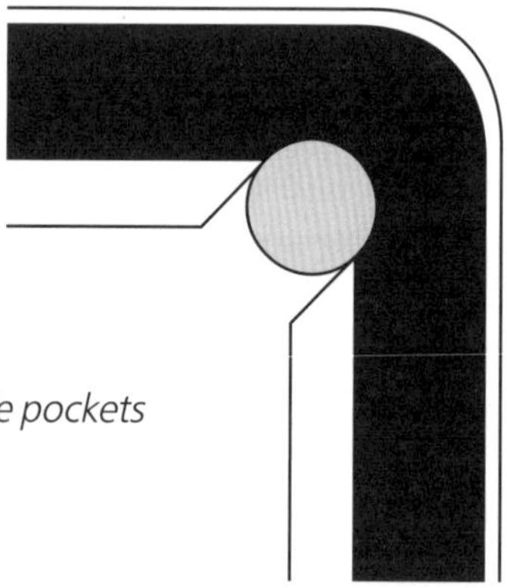

Diagram 37+38 Table pockets

The corner pockets as a rule, have an opening between 11.44cm to 12.75cm, or roughly 4.9 in. to 5.2 in. The side pockets are therefore always roughly 10% wider. A quick and easy method for finding the greatness or tightness a particular tables corner pockets are is to compare the space between two balls that are placed next to each other in the corner pocket. If, for example there is just enough room for two balls as diagram 39 shows, then you are dealing with very tight pockets.

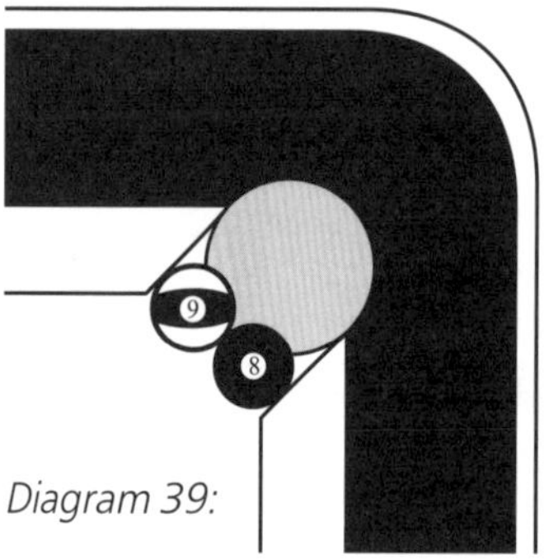

Diagram 39:

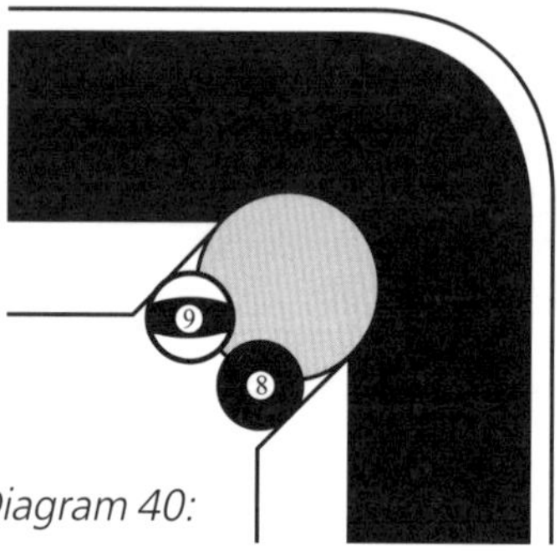

Diagram 40:

Tables with very tight pockets are ideal training tables, because they do not tolerate sloppy play. Usually however, you will find yourself playing on tables whose pocket tolerance is much greater and the space between the two object balls placed next to each other in the pocket is at least one centimeter (1/4 in.) or more (diagram 40).

1.2.5 The cloth

The cloth that covers the pool table must be stretched tightly enough to where bunching of the cloth is no longer possible. By placing the palm of your hand firmly on the table surface, try to slide your hand across the surface. If while doing this, no ruffles in the cloth occur, then the cloth has been stretched correctly. Ruffling of the cloth can cause unwanted movement while positioning your hand by the cue ball, to the cue ball. If this happens during tournament play, it is considered a foul and your opponent comes to the table. Cloth comes in a variety of colors and quality. Red, green, blue and gray have all been tested at one time or another, however those colors, which are used in the billiard industry the most, are yellowish-green and blue-green. Primarily while these two colors resemble grass the most, out of which this sport was originally derived and is found in 90% of all pool halls. The cloth can be made of pure cotton or a mixture of cotton and nylon in which a variety of playing characteristics, toward speed and action in the ball movement, can be observed.

The nylon percentage a cloth has plays a great roll in its playability as well as its long life.

The lesser nylon percentage a wool cloth has, the slower the balls are and the shorter the life-span.

However: If too much nylon in the cloth is present, there may be no stopping the balls, especially if the table surface and balls are warm. Damage to the slate bed of the table surface may also occur. Most tables therefore, use a cotton/nylon or other synthetic mixture somewhere in the area of 70/30 to 90/10 percent.

Pros consider it an advantage when playing on a table, with a new cloth, as the balls tend to slip along easily in the corner pockets at slight angles and the balls breakup easier. Freshly covered rails will let a ball (at lighter angles) slip along at an even lesser angle after hitting it, than during the approach. (See diagram 41)

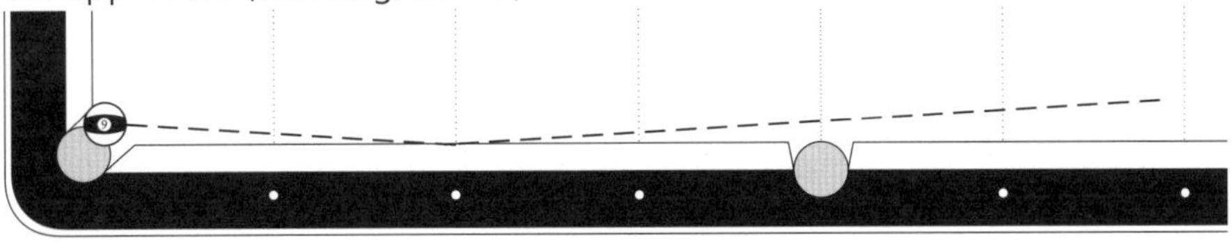

Diagram 41:

Without a doubt, most players will love playing on a good table where the cloth is ideal. On the other hand, a good table can be cruel to you if the cloth is bad. The cloth, depending on how hard and often the table is used, can last between 8, 15 months, and more. During this time the cloth gradually looses its original playing characteristics and will become slower. This aspect affects of course your position playing possibilities on the table surface as well as the rail system itself. The maneuverability and speed of the balls on a table with an older cloth is considerably less lively than compared with a newly covered table. The reason for this is a fine film of soil, consisting of chalk dust, sweat, dust and sometimes baby powder as well. (Baby powder is used for fast relief when hands become sticky or sweaty.) Through time and gravity, these elements impregnate the cloth and cause the balls to move more slowly and react less lively to English. For this reason many poolrooms' vacuum and place, plastic protective coverings over the tables nightly. The soil gathered consequently, can be slightly reduced if one does not chalk a cue or use baby powder directly over the playing field. If traces of baby powder can be readily seen on the table surface, then its use is being overdone. Heavy buildup of chalk dust on the table together with chalk traces on the cue ball and other balls in play can, when rolled together slowly and the chalk traces of different balls meet just right, change the course of a ball being shot in from an angle and magnify the abrasion between these balls drastically.

1.2.6 The slate bed

The playing beds of long ago – during the age of "the royal billiard table" – were made chiefly from massive marble plates. As the game became commercialized, the need for slate was recognized. Slate beds are produced mainly in Italy, are divided in three sections, which when mounted together at its final location are leveled and surface seams are smoothed with putty. No gaps, ridges or indentations should be noticed afterwards. In the beginning, these slates measured between 20 to 25 mm, today they can measure up to 30 mm. The thicker the slate, the stronger the table is. Tables with a slate bed thickness of 19 mm or less or if the playing bed is of another cheaper material, i.e. wood will have weak playing characteristics. For example: When bumping the table accidentally, you can clearly move

Diagram 42: Three slate-bed plates.

the balls and jump shots are extraordinarily difficult because the playing surface "gives in" to the hit and dampers the balls reaction.

1.2.7 Buying a table

Many things should be considered when buying a table, especially if it is for the home. For uncomplicated playing enjoyment and toward the improvement of your ability, make this a serious investment and look for a quality table. If you have trouble in this area, it is always best to get advice from a billiard supply specialist near you and insure that the setup and transport is in the price. Once the table is properly in place, it

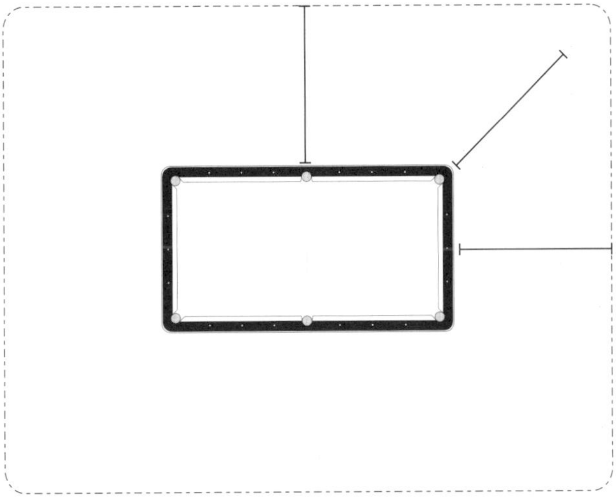

Diagram 43: Minimum table area requirement.

will need readjusting a few weeks later, due to settling, this service should be in the price as well. If this service is not included in the price, you will still need to arrange this, especially if you have carpeting. Nothing can be more disturbing than watching a straight-in ball, over the length of the table, veer off and miss because the table settled more on that side, than equally all around. Slate will bend to a degree. If the table is not completely level, practicing on it will not help you in the long run. How big the table pockets should be depends on what your intentions are. If you intend to present small tournaments for relatives and friends, you may want bigger pockets. If you are of a more selfish nature and are interested primarily in the advancement of your own skills, arrange smaller pockets for your table, as this will refine your aiming technique. Make sure the room you have available is large enough for your table. Rule of thumb: Around the entire pool table, you will need at least a cue length extra, measuring from the outside edge of the table. The best working room around the entire outside edge starts at a cue and a half, 5'3" or 150 cm.

1.3 The balls

1.3.1 History and development

Billiard balls of long ago were originally made of wood. Most were often married with a number of basic problems as the method of production was far from exacting, not to mention difficult and time consuming. The aged hardwood knots and root bases were turned on crude lathes. This process had to be repeated in regular

Diagram 44: Billiard ball set up.

intervals, until the end product was reached and (for that day and age) a good center of balance was achieved. To help you understand the pending problems back then, unless you have played with or produced a set, which most of us have not, needs a little explaining if one is to appreciate our good fortune in the balls of today. Wooden balls would become deformed in time and begin to roll like eggs. They could splinter after a hard collision with another ball and had different weights that would make continuous, perfect positioning simply impossible.

Then the age of ivory was reached, where definite progress over the wooden balls was achieved. Ivory balls were much more elastic and the energy transfer had far more continuity. This meant easier positioning and ball reactions became much more easier to anticipated. Furthermore, the sound of these balls as they clicked together and fell into the pocket, in comparison to wooden balls, became outright soothing to the ear. Ivory however, as does wood, expand and contract to temperature differences. Therefore, it was also with ivory, that they would get „out of round" as the saying went and they also would eventually roll like eggs. Eventually they would chip or crack and even split apart. In time, they would get darker in color and were very sensitive to temperature differences and only a controlled environment could slow this problem. So the problems with ivory were similar to that of wooden balls, in some cases better but in others there was little to no change. Progress in this area was far from perfect. However, the reason for a better material was not due to ivories own drawbacks, but rather because of a constant demand for replacement balls and the growing public interest in the game itself. The wonderful elephants of Africa, primarily due to this sport, were put on the "endangered species" list. This in turn, drove the price of ivory up, making it impossible to commercialize this sport on a broader basis. The search for a cheaper material was badly needed, found and eventually the killing of elephants for their ivory tusks became forbidden. Thank goodness.

1.3.2 Billiard balls of today

Various materials were tested, to include celluloid, metal and even clay, until the industry finally discovered how to harden resin. Through experimentation of different composite mixtures, polyurethane was developed. This was found to be much more durable than ivory. Polyurethane balls had a constant weight, would not deform as ivory would, was not

Playing Accessoires

Diagram 45: Typical pool billiard ball set and its packaging.

temperature or light sensitive to the extremes wood or ivory is. Basically all the negative points ivory had, were positively improved through polyurethane, except that a good ivory cue ball is just a little more livelier.

Polyurethane balls are 2.25 inches in diameter and weigh 6 ounces. There are good composite balls and there are better sets, depending on the independent developing manufacturer to which the ball surface and markings the competing factor is. Therefore, when purchasing, look for clean, clear markings and color. The ball numbers have distinct clear similarities and naturally, no scratches or gouges are observed. A good center of balance can be found in cheaper ball sets as well.

A standard pool billiard ball set consists of 16 balls. One white cue ball and 15 numbered colored balls.

- The balls from 1 to 8 have a solid color, called "solids".
- The balls from 9 to 15 have a colored stripe, to their otherwise white background and are referred to as "stripes".

The numbering of pool balls is coded to their color and is the same internationally, wherever the sport is played. Anyone who refers to color and type will immediately know which numbered ball is meant:

- Ball No. 1/9 = Yellow
- Ball No. 2/10 = Blue
- Ball No. 3/11 = Red
- Ball No. 4/12 = Purple
- Ball No. 5/13 = Orange
- Ball No. 6/14 = Green
- Ball No. 7/15 = Brown
- Ball No. 8 = Black

The stripes share the same color the solids have, except for the 8-ball and the cue ball. A bit of trivial information: If you add 8 to a solid other than the 8 ball itself, you will come up with the same colored striped ball. For instance: The orange 5 plus 8 equals the orange 13.

1.3.3 Maintenance and care

During a tournament, all balls should be clean. However, keeping the cue ball free of chalk marks during a game is not entirely possible. Therefore, the players themselves should take it upon themselves to have the cue ball cleaned regularly. A comfortable way to clean all the balls at once is with a „billiard ball"-polishing machine. Here the balls are rotated and polished at a high RPM. Avoid polishing the balls with wax polishes, as the properties of wax on the balls make their motion deceiving over the cloth and during ball-to-ball contact.

Diagram 46: billiard ball-polishing machine

1.4 Accessories

Playing Accessoires

1.4.1 Chalk

Diagram 47:

Because the abrasion between a blank leather cue tip and the cue ball is very limited, chalk has become an important accessory to the game. This of course, when applied to the leather tip, increases the abrasion between these two surfaces and allows one to strike the cue ball far outside its center. Miscuing – which happens every now and again – rarely propels the cue ball in the expected direction. The leather and/or ferrule can become damaged after miscuing due to the lack of chalk. On the other hand, a "chalk dust spot" on the ball surface that contacts another ball just right, may also negatively affect a games progress, because "the one" can drag "the other" off an intended course.

1.4.1.1 Effects of chalk

Chalk is normally blue in color and contains calcium carbonate, silica sand and other abrasives and dyes. One of these cubes should always rest in easy reach upon the rail. The reason for chalk by now is of course clear. However, during the explanation earlier in which, the abrasion between these two surfaces is magnified with chalk, if you chalk your cue often, which you should (once after each shot, is not uncommon) refrain from chalking over the table and always lay the chalk right side up on the rail. This may not sound like much, but if you clean the cloth and balls regularly, you can play much longer before strange things start to happen.

1.4.1.2 Method of chalking

Chalking the tip should not make a lot of noise. Use simple circular motions to the leather surface until its face is completely covered. Be careful not to mark the white ferrule. One does not need to chalk after every shot, however for those shots where you need to hit outside of the cue ball center, it is strongly recommended. This is the least you can do to protect against miscuing. The most important area to chalk on the tip is its outermost face, (see diagram 48). The reason here may be clear. When the cue ball is struck near its center, the contact point is a small degree greater than when struck outside of this area. This contact surface becomes harder to grab (especially during power strokes) the further away from the center one hits the cue ball until miscuing occurs, (see diagram 49, in this case upwards). Actually, one does not need to chalk the center of the cue tip at all, providing your stroke and delivery is decent, because the delivery normally travels straight through that part of the ball. For the good and experienced player, chalking the cue has become a systematic, unconscious ritual. They will chalk often, thoroughly and lightly, using this phase of the game to study situations or to get their rhythm developed or both. One can observe many forms when watching experienced players. If you are looking for method, it is best to observe good players in action, maybe copy someone you admire; we will leave this up to you.

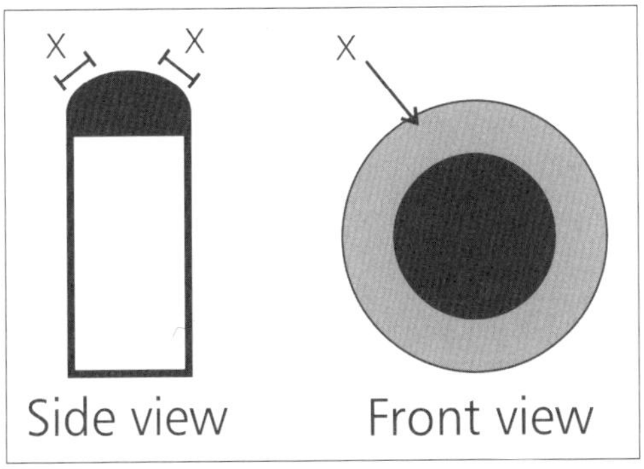

Diagram 48: X = the important part of the leather tip that must always be saturated with chalk.

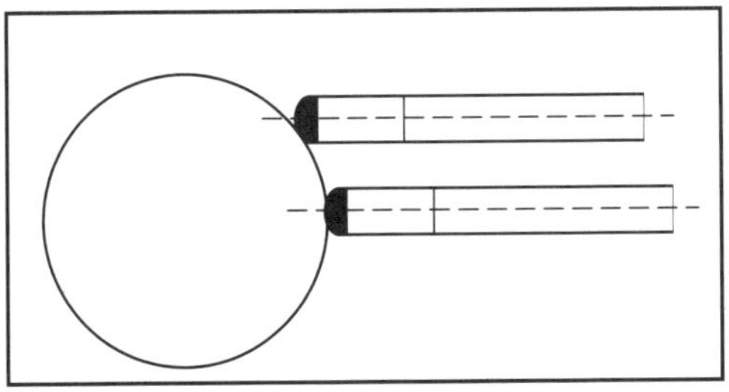

Diagram 49:

At this point, we would like to describe an area of the cue ball all players wish to avoid. This being the last third of an inch or 1 cm ring of the cue balls "outer limits". For lack of a better word, we will describe this as the "slip-zone" and where miscuing will always occur no matter how well the tip is prepared. The "assault" or grabbing surface becomes less than a fraction of that inside and away from the slip-zone. Now that you realize how big the "slip zone" actually is, it might become easier to avoid.

We hope that all of you, who are still learning in life, appreciate the eloquence of this sport and realize the worth of the "good manners" you have already learned. There are some unsaid rules to which are worth explaining to those who are unaware.

You may have already noticed in the course of time, that a cube of chalk may wear down but does not evaporate. This was also described in chapter 1.2.5. A common practice among well-bred players is that they avoid chalking their cue directly over the table (enough chalk is being spread after the cue ball is struck) and when finished chalking, they place the chalk right-side-up on the table. Too much chalk dust on the table may rob you eventually of that last half inch you needed, to get "position" and by always placing the chalk "right side up" on the rail, you eventually know, unconsciously and without looking, where the opening is and at the same time avoid spilling unnecessary chalk residue on the rail as well.

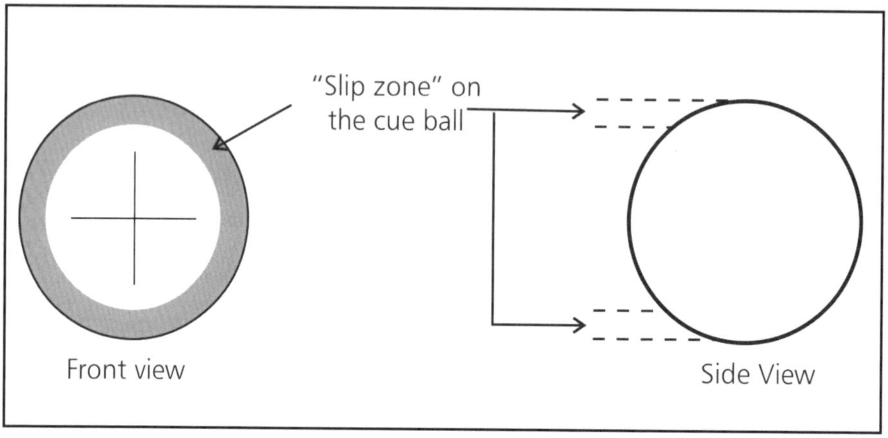

Diagram 50: Hitting the cue ball anywhere inside the slip zone will cause one to muscae, regardless of how well the cue tip was initially prepared or groomed.

1.4.2 The rack

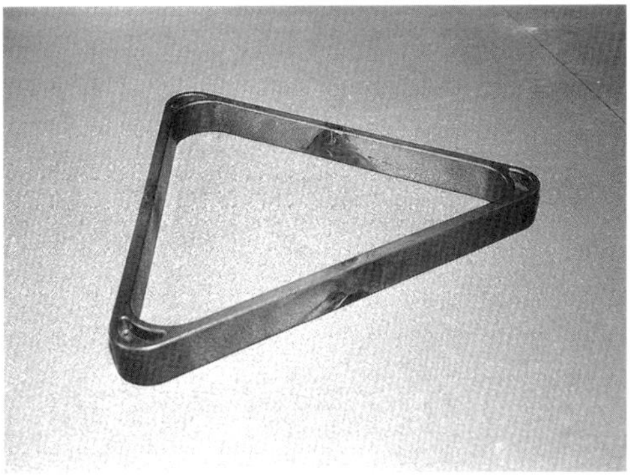

Diagram 51:

In order to set 15 balls up the same way every time and keep from passing perspiration from the palms of your hands to the balls at a minimum, one should use the help of the racking-triangle or simply "the rack". This easy to use accessory is normally made of sturdy, durable plastic or wood and both have roughly the same thickness. Plastic racks of the thinner version are not as good as they bend and deform much too easily. All types however, should have no sharp edges as this could damage the cloth. The racking of the balls should be fast and effective, making sure all balls are "touching" one another in the same outlined place on the table.

Doing this always will certainly make it easier to rack the balls in the future. However, if the establishment where you normally play pool has players who rack their games with less care, then racking the balls exactly together will be a matter of trial and error. Try rubbing your hand over the racking area to remove dust or chalk particles. If you still have a problem keeping the balls together, consider tapping that "problem child" lightly in place with the help of your opponent, if he is willing to help you. It is important for the games constant character, that all of the balls in the setup be touching as the balls spread much better after the break as well as normally every experienced players wish.

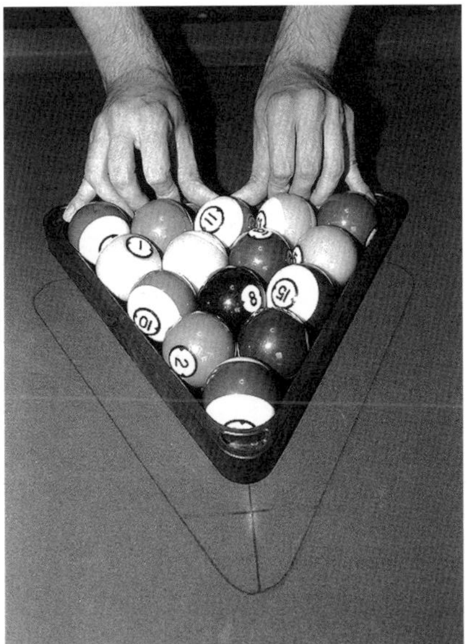

Diagram 52: Racking up the balls.

1.4.3 The mechanical bridge (crutch)

Playing Accessoires

Shots where the normal, comfortable, free stroking ability is strongly limited, help in the form of the mechanical bridge is usually provided, sometimes lovingly addressed as the "grandma". For example: The shot you wish to make is simply too far down the other end and on the wrong side of the table. The makeup in the design of the crutch is similar to that of a garden rake (to which it is sometimes referred to, i.e. the rake) and is normally somewhat shorter in length than a normal cue stick. The flanged head of the crutch is designed to support the cue shaft on a couple of levels, depending on the action one wishes to give to the cue ball for that particular situation. The crutch comes in a variety of designs and materials. Many players avoid the use of the mechanical bridge,

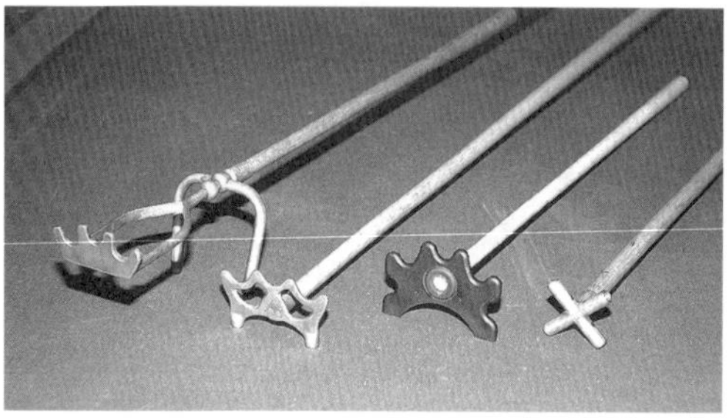

Diagram 53: Various types of mechanical bridges.

Diagram 54: Normal bridge

Diagram 55: Elevated bridge

as the stroking technique is somewhat different than during normal play. For this reason, ambidextrous techniques in the cue use can become highly developed. To develop your other hand will cost you twice as long to develop your general skill in pool than it will take to master the use of the mechanical bridge. Whereby, those of whom who have developed their weak hand from the beginning can eventually develop a decided advantage over the mechanical bridge in security. One can form a closed bridge eventually and thereby be able to develop a stronger stroke. Either way you decide, one thing is certain, both methods require practice.

1.4.4 Talcum or baby powder

Diagram 56:

These types of powders stop the shaft from sticking to the guiding portion of the bridge hand. One should apply this powder to that portion of the bridge-hand where the cue shaft normally comes to. For best results: Take a 2 X 2 inch, flat piece of cardboard, or similar, and lay this on a flat surface away from the pool table. Pour a small amount of powder on the cardboard. By rolling a portion of the bridge range of the shaft through this small pile of powder, it will inherently cause the powder to stick to the shaft. Now, form your closed bridge fingers around the powder sticking to the shaft and stroke your cue as you would normally do during play. However, stroke "in the air" and away from the pool table. Banging your hand against the shaft lightly will remove any excess residue.

However, using the palm of your hand rather than the flat piece of cardboard will inherently leave white palm prints all over the pool table which, in many establishments is frowned upon. The properties of baby or talcum powder (although not as extreme as chalk-dust) will offer more negative reactions to the games' progress than positive.

Notice:

2. Stance and grip

The proper stance for a given situation, together with the correct grip for the bridge hand, will invariably allow the stroking hand to move freely, comfortably and effectively. A fact, which is one of the most important basic abilities, if a higher level of play is desired. The correct stance and grip for both bridge and stroking hand should always be the same for all types of shots encountered on the pool table.

2.1 The stance

The most basic and important rule of the stance is: If I am comfortable while stroking, then I have a good stance.

2.1.1 the ideal stance

Because not everybody has the same build or height, it is quite difficult to explain the ideal stance for each individual. In short, there is no such thing as an ideal stance! However, there are important general "Points of interest", which will eventually lead one to their own, individual, ideal stance if followed consequently.

These general points of interest have been crystallized after watching the techniques of the "Cream of the crop" by professional trainers for many decades: The one professional player has a good stance, the other has a good aiming system, then another has a great stroking technique. These points were then generalized as they were found to be sensible and easy to explain. Therefore, the following general points of interest for your own individual size will help you to develop your own ideal stance.

How one stands at the table during a particular situation is immaterial as long as these three points are always present:

- A comfortable stance; weight balance is 50:50 to each side of you,
- An effective aiming technique; the chin and elbow are

directly over the cue and,

- Stroke the cue straight; the cue misses the body during the follow-through.

Stance and grip

The beginner should first learn from the majority of shots where the above "points of interest" are easily applied, to learn comfort, effectiveness and freedom. Which means: 7 out of 10 situations should hold similar opportunities for the adaptation of an ideal stance. However, in order to market these "comfortable areas" to shoot from, one must be able to aim and stroke effectively consistently and why it is so important to address the table correctly consistently.

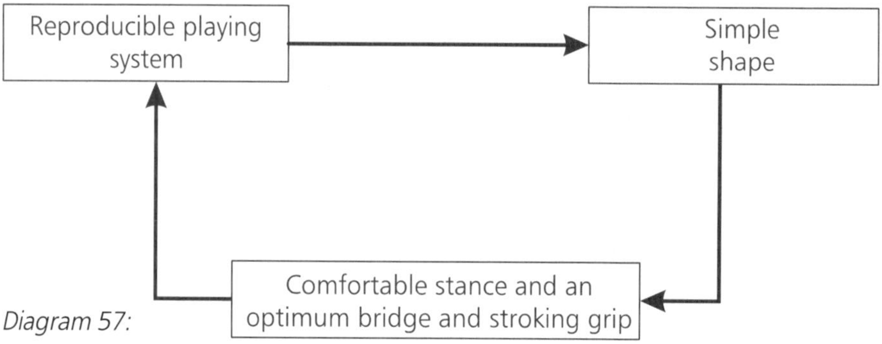

Diagram 57:

Making the shot and getting shape for the next, can only be continually produced after becoming accustomed perfectly to your ideal stance.

2.1.1.1 A comfortable stance

In all cases of a comfortable stance, the weight distribution to both sides of you is equally distributed. Notwithstanding, whether both legs are bent equally or the front leg is bent and the rear is straight or one needs to stretch over the table, to reach and apply the delivery, whereby you will

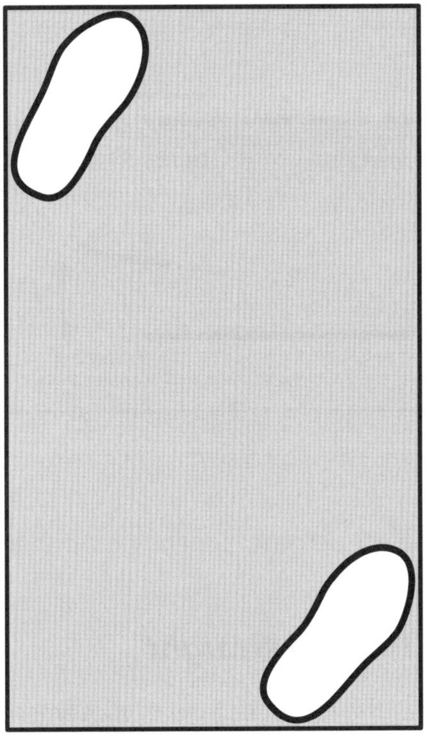

Diagram 58:

tend to lift one of your legs in the process to get that extra inch or two. Incorrect weight distribution will inevitably lead to early exhaustion in concentration, especially when you need to pace yourself in a tournament, which requires that you concentrate effectively to the excess of several hours. Therefore, cultivate your comfort and play well longer. Good balance at the table is described at best, when one can position the feet similar to the example in diagram 58. Adaptation and refinement of a good, comfortable stance during difficult situations, where the delivery is consequent, effective and productive is a hallmark of every great player. Consequently, if you can get comfortable with whatever it is you like to do, you can eventually become great at it.

2.1.1.2 Effective aiming technique

Effective aiming technique as seen from above, requires that your warm-up strokes are as level to the table as possible and straight. Extending your straight warm-up stroke into a straight follow-through stroke, will be the difference in knowing whether you have propelled the cue ball into the object ball as you expected, or realize during its course that things are not going to turnout as you had hoped. Your disillusion will become immediate and progressive, unless you understand how important it is to bridge the extension between warm-up and follow-through perfectly.

One of the important reasons for keeping the cue as level as possible, is this allows the eye level to be held low as well. For every centimeter the butt of the cue is raised, 1% to 2 % failure is added. If a player continuously raises the butt of his cue for a difference of one foot, they have an unnec-

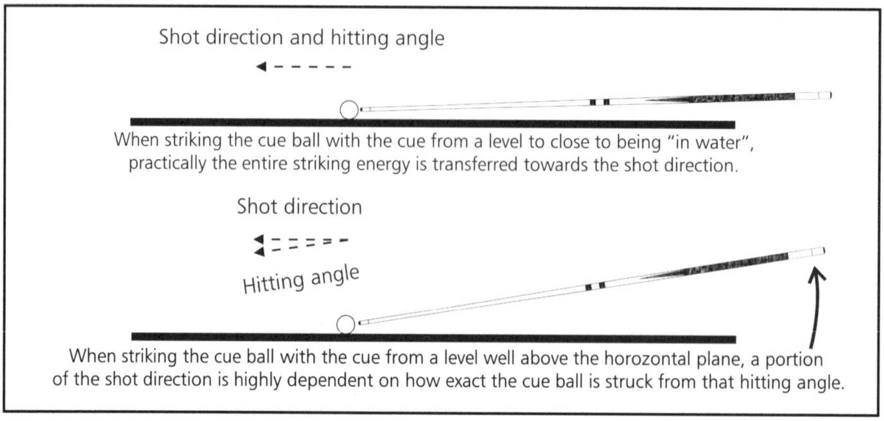

Diagram 60:

essary failure quotient between 15 and 30 percent, depending on their ability.

2.1.1.3 Freedom to stroke the cue straight

This must be accomplished, so that the cue in its area of movement does not have to avoid any obstacles. Be it the hip or other portion of the upper torso, due to improperly addressing the situation at hand or because the room area in which the pool table is situated is quite small for normal play.

For example: the wall, a piece of furniture or a support pillar is inside the minimum working range around the outside edge of the table and continuously impairs normal freedom of play. No serious player would think of coming to a place like this very often, at least not to practice. Such occurrences and/or situations naturally have a negative influence to the "general points of interest" which need to be sot after in order to produce satisfying results continuously.

2.1.2 Feet and leg position

Diagram 61 illustrates a good example where the feet should be placed when addressing the cue ball for this typical shot situation. Depending on your height, shorter or larger, the feet position will move diagonally either closer together or farther apart. The point here is, the feet should in all

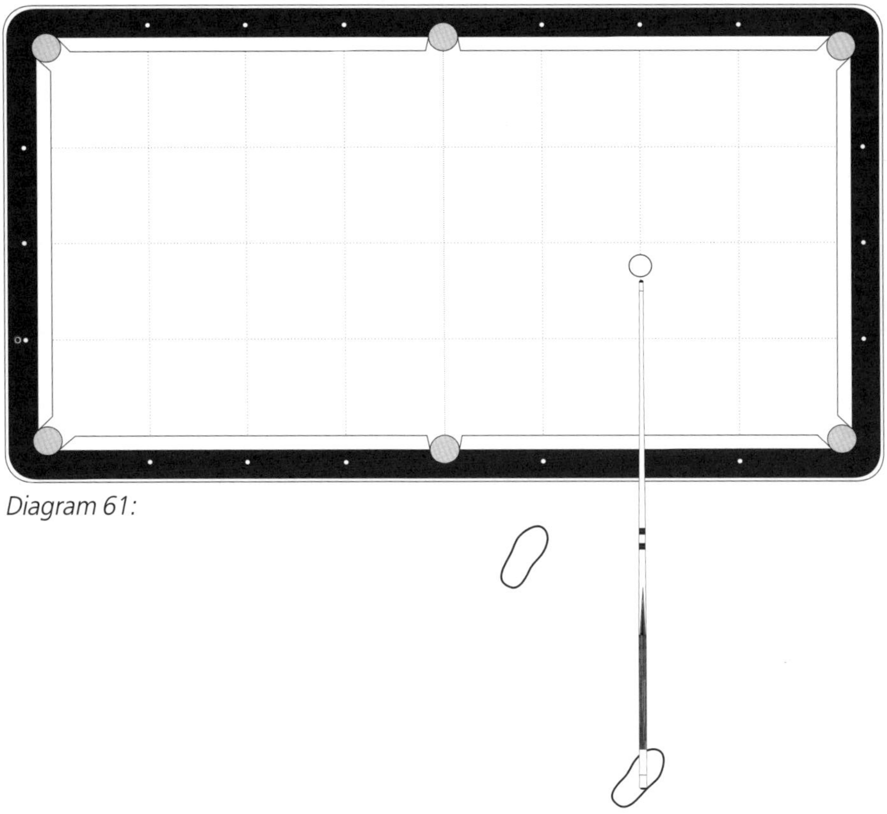

Diagram 61:

cases be far enough apart, that if someone where to shove you lightly, you would not have to take a step to catch your balance. Think of this as though you are standing inside and against the boundaries of a comfortable rectangle, see diagram 58.

Stance and grip

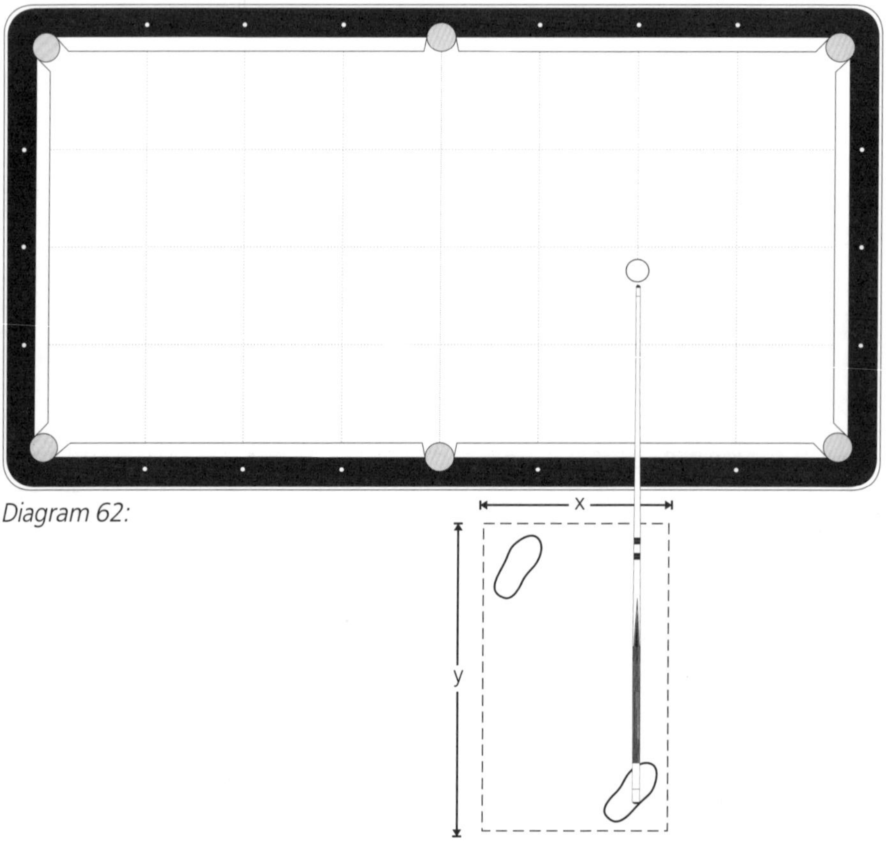

Diagram 62:

The taller the player, the greater the distance between x and y.

Should your feet placement be similar to those in diagram 63, you may be addressing the table wrong, or maybe you are adapting to your environment. However, if you are comfortable, then you are standing correct at the table.

In diagram a) and b), we see the players addressing parallel to the table. Typical for snooker players, especially in diagram b), the hip needs to

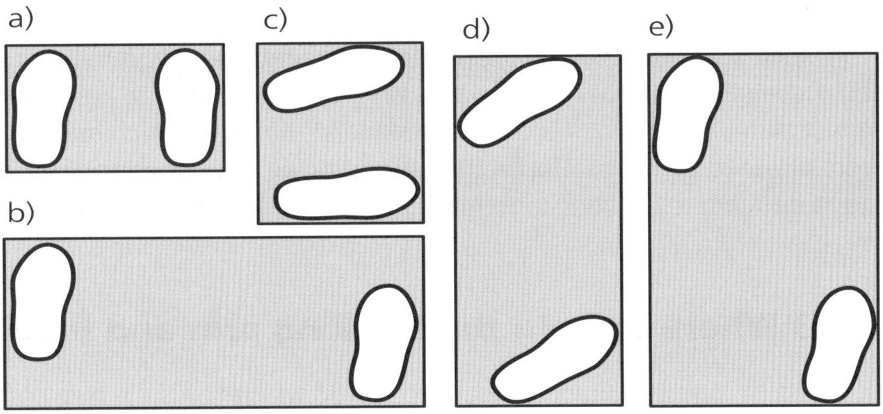

Diagram 63:

be moved to the left or right, depending if they are left or right handed or the stroking hand will graze the hip, to which the player must always avoid.

In diagram c) and d), the player seems to be standing on a rail or they need to play around a slight beer belly. If that is the reason and they are comfortable, this could be a good stance as well.

In diagram e), though this stance is quite stable, notice the feet positioning as they are similar to those in diagram a) and b). Your weight distribution should be divided equally, where both knees are slightly bent or the

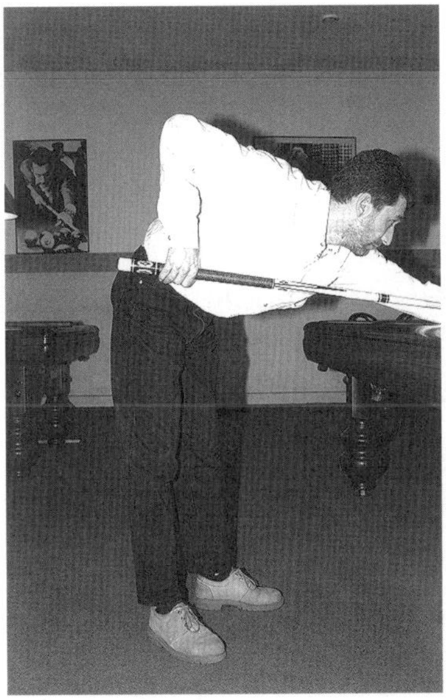

Diagram 64:

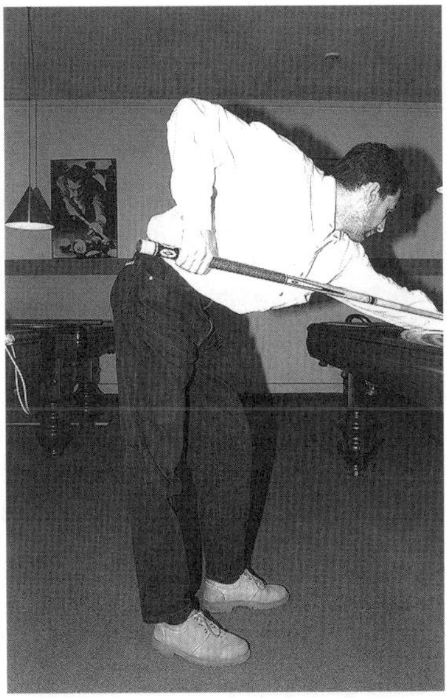

Diagram 65:

front knee is slightly bent and the rear leg is straight. (See diagram 64 and 65). Depending on your height to the table, you may decide to keep your legs straight. Either way you choose to stand at the table, which may vary from player to player, comfort is the key and as we mentioned earlier will play a deciding roll to your concentration level at this sport.

2.1.3 Where to hold the stroking arm and hand

The stroking arm/hand, is that part of you which holds the butt portion of the cue. Usually right-handers will grab this portion of the cue with their right hand. Taller players will find that their grip is farther back, sometimes behind the wrap portion of the cue and therefore further away from the balancing point, than those who are shorter or as in children. Important is, where your normal range is for your height and where your grip should be before the movement or warm-up stroking begins. There are many methods of teaching this to beginners. From finding the balancing point on the cue and then spreading the thumb and forefinger toward the butt-end, up to complicated measuring of the forearm and height. It is easy for one to get a bit carried away. However, we believe and will attempt to describe an even simpler and more effective avenue of approach.

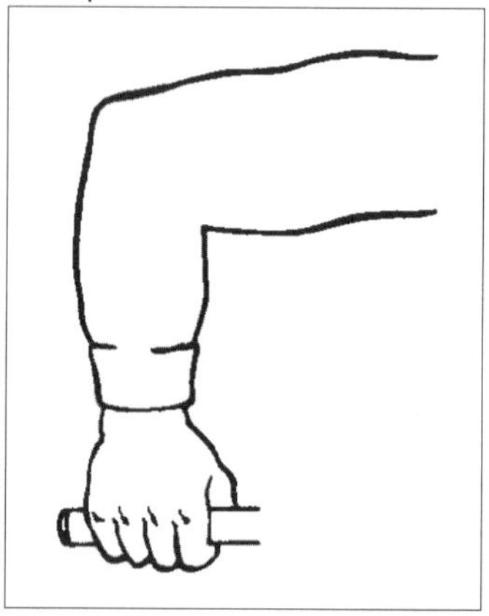

Diagram 66: Stroking arm at right angles from the elbow to

Shortly before the tip touches the cue ball, your stroking hand and forearm should hang vertically and straight down from the elbow. (See diagram 67)

Diagram 67:

You should hold this position of the stroking arm as close to 90° as possible. The important thing here is that the forearm can hang in this position comfortable and relaxed. Because the length of the cue, to the height of the person doesn't always match perfectly, keeping this right angle in the stroking arm may to a degree or two be impaired, something which can be well adapted to and therefore not too important.

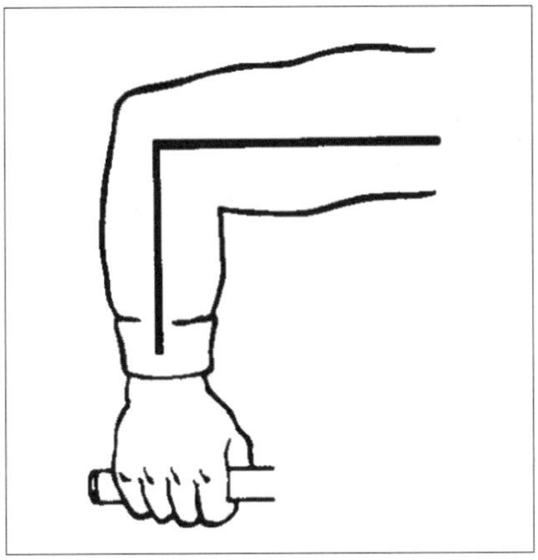
Diagram 68:

Stance and grip

When the grip zone has been established for normal bridges, beginners should mark this spot on the cue with a rubber band, as this will help them to grip correctly and continuously. (Highlighted in white, in example 69, place it just in front of the gripping thumb and forefinger)

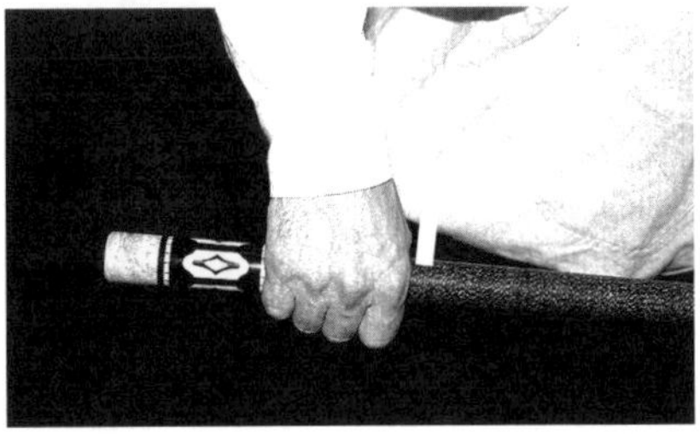
Diagram 69:

One advantage in having the forearm hang perpendicular to the ground is that your forearm, at this position, requires no energy to hang there. Therefore, the force used to move backwards and forwards can be duplicated for both directions from that position.

Diagram 70:

Gripping the cue too far forward as shown in example 71, can in some cases, especially when the elbow on up does not move, cause one to move through the cue ball improperly or not enough. This will lead to an improper follow-through (unless desired) in almost all cases. To achieve a level fol-

Stance and grip

low-through still, you must drop the elbow to the cue, however the tip should never end up any higher than where the cue ball was struck. Beginners however, should always strive for a stiff upper arm, and this causes the cue tip to dive towards the table surface.

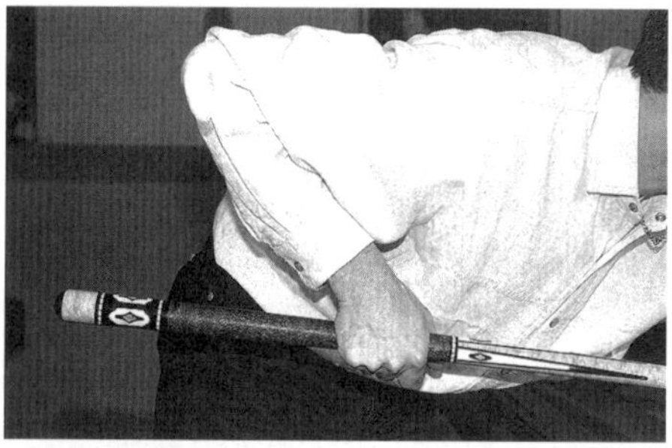

Diagram 71:

Many pros, while not gripping their cue as far forward as in example 71, use a form of this method regularly. They do not get away from breaking their upper arm, to achieve follow-through to the cue ball, but with such perfection continuously, one can hardly attempt to question their technique. We are talking about very experienced players, which, for a beginner is quite difficult to learn. Then, the pro will always grip his cue at exactly the right point for every shot and stroke the ball – something a beginner or hobby player needs more time to learn.

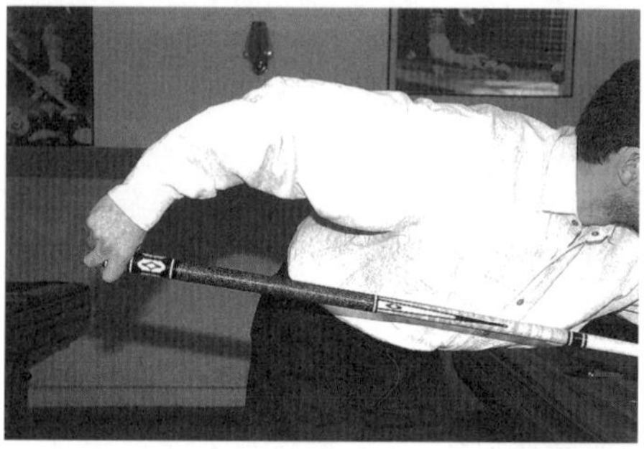

Diagram 72:

One very common mistake among beginners however, is that they do just the opposite. Many will start out holding their cue too far to the rear as in example 72. In order to understand that this is a strong disadvantage, we need to explain what we are trying to describe by example. In Diagram 73, Mr. Sander is attempting to throw a ball as far as he can, starting from this position, standing against a wall. One can readily see that there is no room to "wind-up" in order to throw the ball far. This same principle applies, if the beginner holds the cue as demonstrated in the previous example. You need room to the rear to measure and gather the speed needed otherwise, you are just guess-

Diagram 73:

ing. You should never guess, it is better to calculate with much confidence and for a beginner this may take more time than normal, but if the result is important to you and you guess, you learn very little.

The stroking arm should always be situated, so there is freedom of movement, but not so far away as to keep from getting comfortable. Then, the elbow should always be directly over the cue – smaller people and children exempted – in this way the cue can be guided straight, naturally and easily.

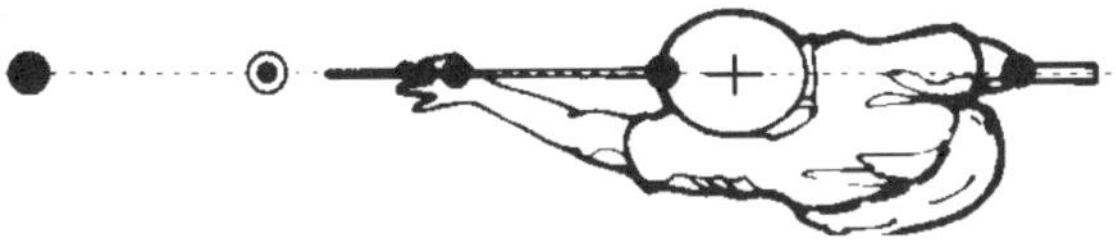

Diagram 74: Source: Billiard – The official rules & records book.

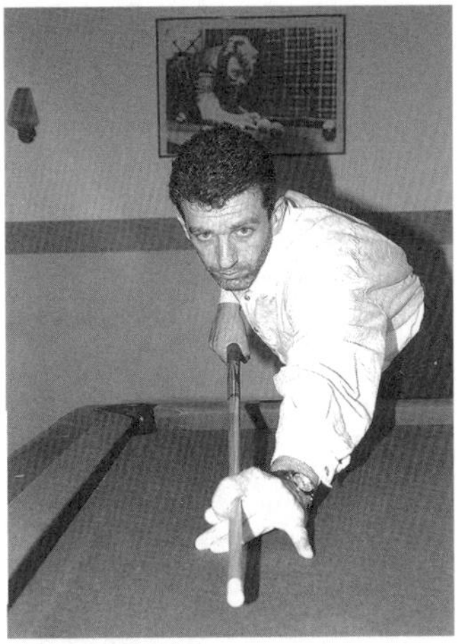

Diagram 75:

2.1.4 Head and torso position

Diagram 76:

Diagram 77:

The head should be situated so that the chin to the cue is no more than five and a half inches or a palm and a half apart. The cue – for normal shots – should be held as level to the table as possible. Pros all hold their chin between Zero and 5.5 inches above the cue; so pick what is right for you.

Stance and grip

Diagram 78:

However, during very strong strokes - for example: the break - getting "too low" on the ball when aiming, may impair a good follow-through. Although getting down low is considered good for normal shots, during very strong strokes one needs to allow room for the follow-through, as this motion will inevitably cause the cue to rise toward the chin and torso. Therefore, give yourself just a little more room during such a shot.

To get the best site picture possible, refrain from cocking your head to the side, as in example 78. Keep your eyes level, as there are some good reasons for doing so. First, when tilting the head to the side the depth perception becomes impaired and second, this will take one longer to learn speed control. It also makes it difficult to judge angles correctly as depth perception is an absolute requirement when aiming the cue ball to the object ball correctly. Another good reason for keeping the eyes level, this may help keep you from getting a stiff neck.

Some players actually aim so low as to rub their chin periodically against the cue while stroking. They do this to make certain that their aiming technique remains the same and that a change in the distance between the cue and the table or the cue and the chin will be readily noticed and adjusted to. However, such a technique will not always allow the beginner to keep the upper portion of the "stroking" arm stiff. (The advantages or a stiff upper arm is explained in more depth, in the upcoming chapters.) During a full follow-through, the cue will rub harder against the chin causing you to either drop your upper arm or you make the big mistake of raising your head. Raising the head after shooting a ball, does not allow one to "register" the reason for making or missing a shot correctly. Holding the initial eye level is very important before and during the shot, as this is also a good way to help develop your judgment.

The cue is held as close to the body as possible, without it bothering the complete straight stroking movement. Example 79 and 80 represent two extreme aiming stances, too far away and too close to the body. Both are considered disadvantages for learning purposes and either hinders a complete free and straight stroke or gives the player the feeling the cue is not entirely under their complete control.

Diagram 79: too far away and...

Diagram 80: too close to the hip.

However, as extreme as this may be, there are professionals (not many) who have mastered these extreme-aiming techniques successfully. They are of course, exceptions to the rule. The point we want to make however, is that there are sensible reasons to hold your stance more upright than normal, for certain shots:

- ♦ The break shot can benefit more when you stand with more room between the cue and torso. Here are a few tips when breaking:
  - Raise the body a foot higher than normal
  - Lengthen the bridge to the cue ball 2 to 3 inches more and
  - Draw the cue back slowly and completely back to the bridge hand

  Most professionals have taken the time to practice just the

break. Then the professional knows how much of an advantage he has if his break is continuously successful.

- Standing a little higher over the cue may help in other cases as well. For example, when the object ball is inside an inch or two from the cue ball, one is not looking only to where the object ball has to go, but where the cue ball and object ball need to touch in order to get the object ball moving in the right direction. In diagram 81, the object ball is laying roughly an inch away and the angle to the pocket is greater than 20°. In this case, it may be easier to first realize and then observe the contact points from a more elevated point of view while aiming.

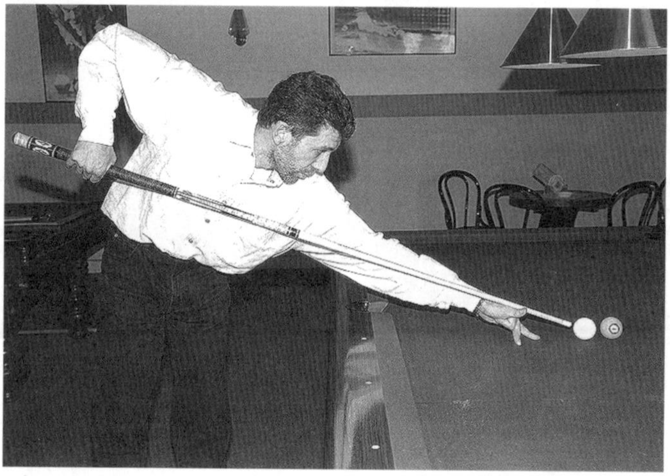

Diagram: 81

2.2 Gripping

The most sensible, effective and comfortable stance is only as good as the proper grip on the cue for the situation at hand. The bridge and stroking hand, if held wrong, will cripple any progress you may be in search of.

2.2.1 the bridge hand

The bridge hand can be formed in two basic ways:

a) The open bridge

b) The closed bridge

2.2.1.1 the open bridge

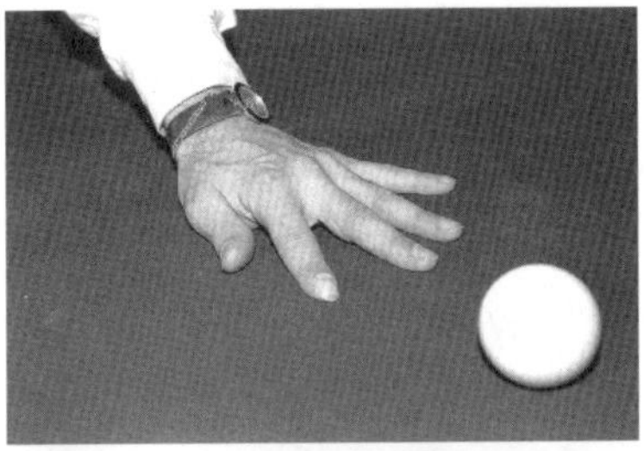

a) Place the palm of your hand, flat with spread fingers, on the table surface.

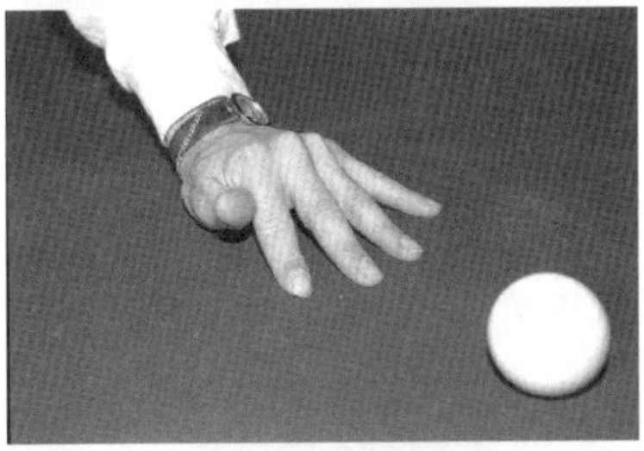

b) Raising the knuckles lightly from the table surface only,

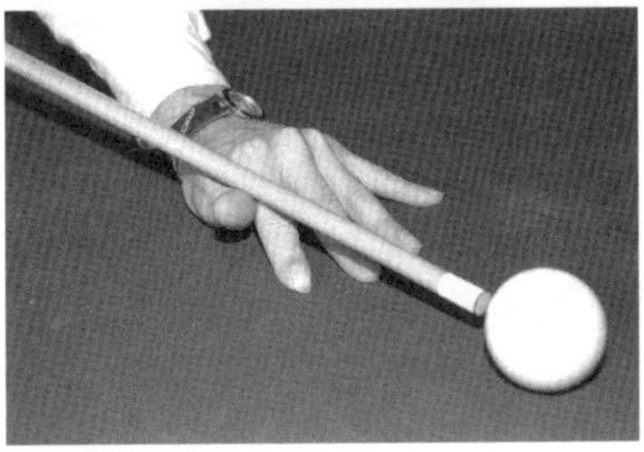

c) Bring the first joint of your thumb to the forefinger between its knuckle and first joint and form a small "V" with the thumb and knuckle of the forefinger.

Diagram 82 - 84:

By placing the shaft of the cue in this "V" of the open bridge you have formed, moving the cue back and forth should cause no uncomfortable feeling but rather glide smoothly and trouble-free and no stickiness should be felt.

Depending on how high or low one wishes to strike the face of the cue ball, raising or lowering the knuckles of the bridge hand offer easy accessibility.

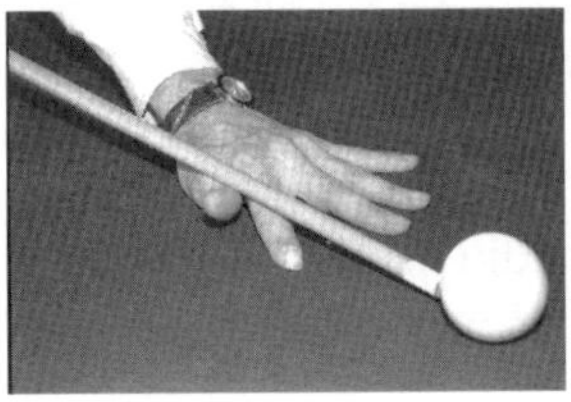
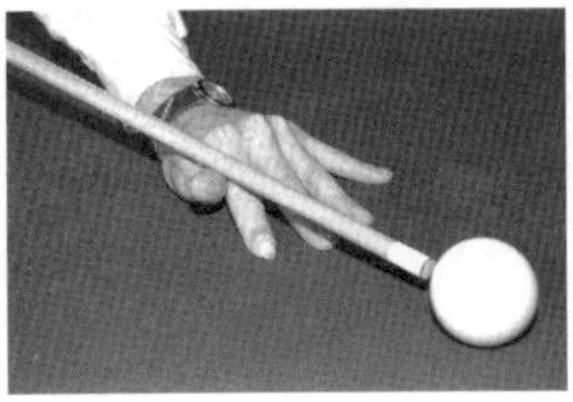
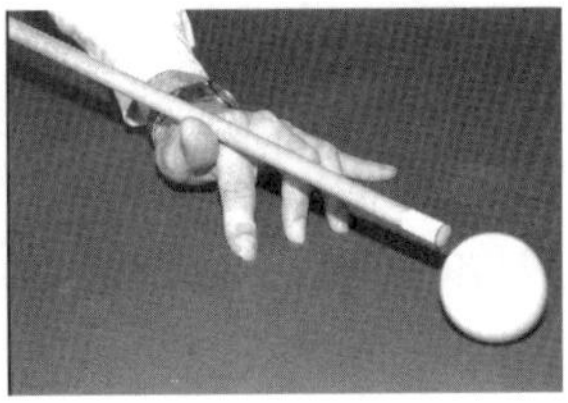

Diagram 85 - 87:

Open bridge advantages:

- One has an unobstructed view of the cue shaft while aiming and this helps greatly, especially during long shots.
- The open bridge is ideal when aiming over other balls, as this technique is the sturdiest and most dependable.
- There is no situation during play where the open bridge cannot be used; in some cases, it is the only sensible choice.

Open bridge disadvantages:

- The shaft stays in the "V" of the open bridge only through the "might" of gravity. When utilizing the open bridge an evenly tempered stroke is always required, not wild or rushed as this may cause the shaft to "jump up" and strike the face of the cue ball wrongly, miscue or just miss the cue ball entirely!
- For those who are somewhat smaller in height and children, care must be taken not to grip the cue on or around the balancing point, as the cue will "jump up" more readily when using the open bridge. (See chapter 1.1.2.1 the balancing point)

2.2.1.2 The closed bridge

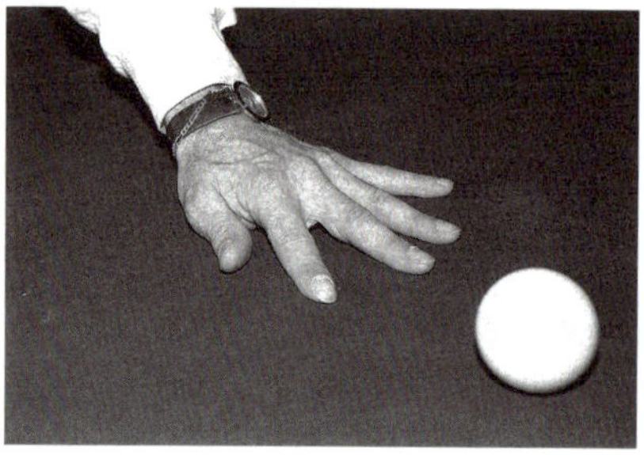

Diagram 88

a) Place the palm of your hand, flat with spread fingers, on the table surface.

b) Raising the finger knuckles lightly from the table surface and the complete forefinger,

c) Press the thumb to the first joint of the middle finger underneath the raised forefinger and form the small "V".

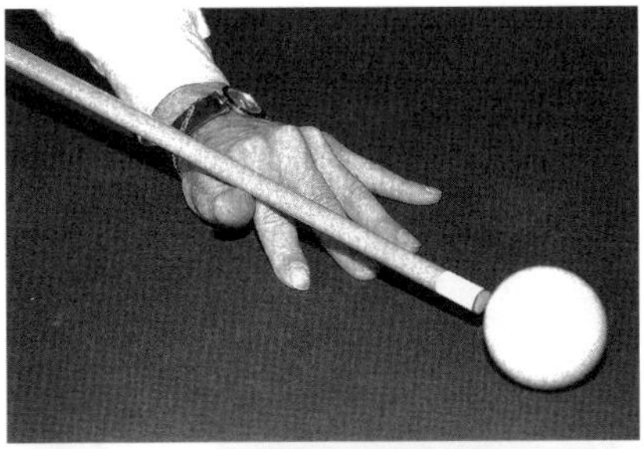

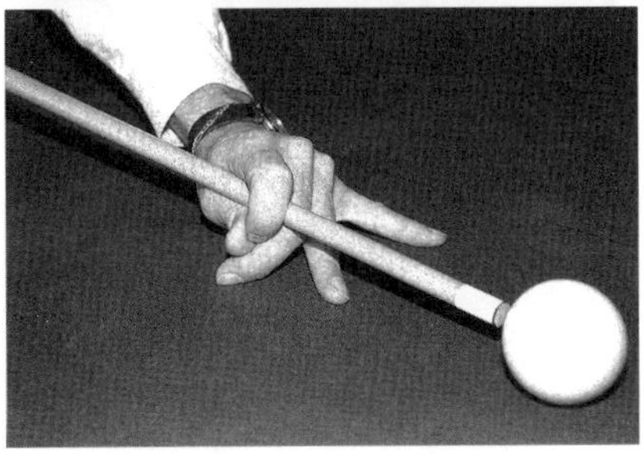

Diagram 88-90

d) Create a closed loop by connecting the tip of the forefinger to the end of the thumb after placing the shaft on top of the small "V" formed earlier.

This is the basic form of the closed bridge and you may find it a little too loose or a little tight or maybe you get along with it from the start. However, those who have trouble with the closed bridge in the beginning should realize that it can be adapted to, but is not an immediate requirement. The important point here is, the closed bridge must form snugly around the entire shaft and still allow the cue to glide through it smoothly and easily. A "moisture-free" shaft and bridge hand will help you enormously here. Wash and "dry" your hands thoroughly and/or clean the cue shaft and start again from the beginning.

The following example demonstrates how the height to the cue ball is adjusted; for follow, stop and draw shots.

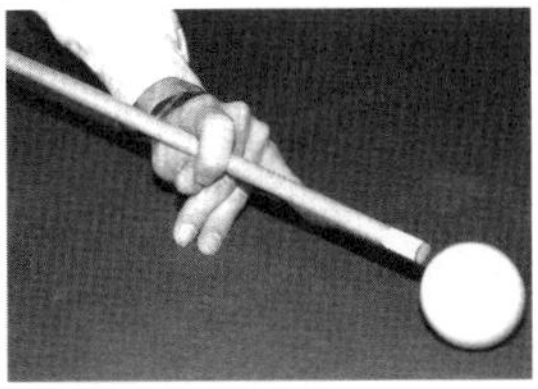

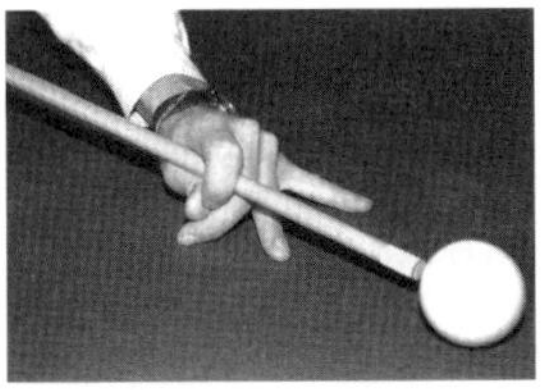

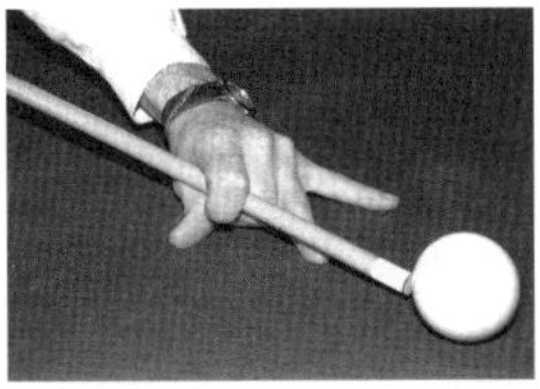

Diagram 91-93

Keeping the heel of the bridge hand and the fingertips on the table surface constantly, raising or lowering the knuckle of the middle finger will allow one to vary the height to the cue ball.

The advantages of a closed bridge:

- The shaft movement is confined to its preferred level of contact on the cue ball, which gives added security during aiming.
- The shaft is unable to "jump up" after the follow through

is completed; one hits therefore, that portion of the cue ball surface more exactly.

- Because the shaft movement is confined, smaller persons to children are able to grip the cue on or around the balancing point without fear that the shaft will "jump up".
- Power draw shots are sometimes more effective with a closed bridge.
- Some form of the closed bridge is helpful for a power break shot.

The disadvantages of a closed bridge:

- Because the forefinger wraps around the upper portion of the shaft, the overhead view of the entire shaft is partially impaired. This can be deceiving when aiming for a long shot.
- It can be extremely difficult to impossible to correctly aim over other balls at the cue ball. Sturdiness and security is lost as soon as the heel of the hand leaves the table and can get worse as some try to balance on three fingers or less!
- There is also the limitation when the need to "reach the shot" or when shooting the cue ball away from the rail is required. At this point, the closed bridge becomes increasingly uncomfortable and/or unstable.

B.C.A. Trainer, Jack H. Koehler related to us in his book, one reason why many professionals may have retained the closed bridge, as follows: "My theory is: Most professionals have started shooting pool at a very early age and therefore needed a closed bridge as they would invariably hold the cue on or around the balancing point. As they grew older, this accustomed form of gripping the shaft was just naturally adhered to."

Those of you who have problems with the closed bridge will automatically develop the open bridge. However, as one begins to discover the "extreme shots", the development of the closed bridge will help you to execute these shots with more comfort and security.

2.2.1.3 The bridge length

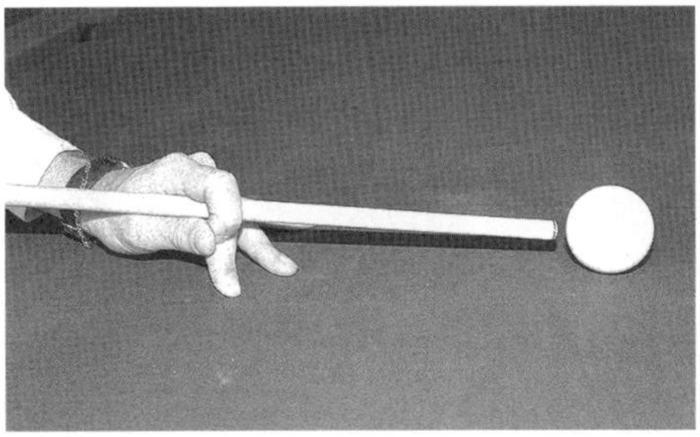

Diagram 94

The bridge length for most pros is 8 to 10 in. unless the shot dictates otherwise. A bridge length any less than this and the possible power for the shot will begin to weaken. A bridge length any more than this magnifies any impurities your stroking hand holds (if any), during the follow-through. Shorter players often have a longer bridge length than taller players as this helps shorter players see the aiming point on the cue ball more clearly. However, the best bridge length for you should hold these two important points.

Diagram 95 - 96

1. Shortly before the leather tip makes contact with the cue ball, your arm at the elbow should hang perpendicular to the ground.

2. The bridge length should never be so short, that when the stroking hand declares the back swing, the cue falls out of the bridge hand.

Up to a quarter table length, the follow through should be at least as long as the back swing for soft shots. The back swing always defines the minimum length of the follow-through. Beginners, following our advise in keeping a stiff upper arm, will find playing inside of this range, everything will happen as we have described, except that soft shots are not normal shots – medium shot are normal shots. However, you will find that your feel for a soft shot will come better if you draw back 2 inches and follow-through 2 inches.

The normal length of the bridge ranges between 8 and 10 inches for most players.

Two extreme examples are shown in the following four photographs and are not needed for normal play.

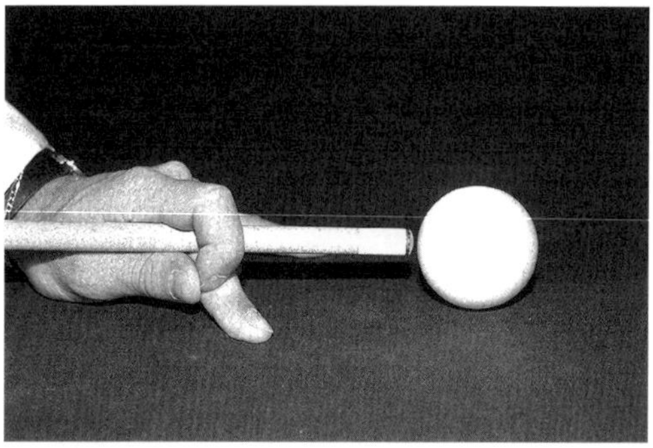

Diagram 97: very short bridge

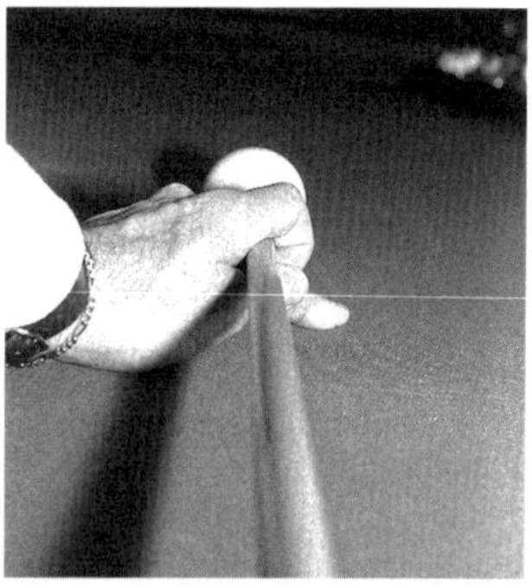

Diagram 98:

The upper left example shows a very short bridge to the cue ball. The advantage of a short bridge is to contact the cue ball with the tip at a more precise spot. Small rudder motions in the stroking arm, either to the left or to the right, up or down will be in a very little circle on the cue ball. (see example 98).

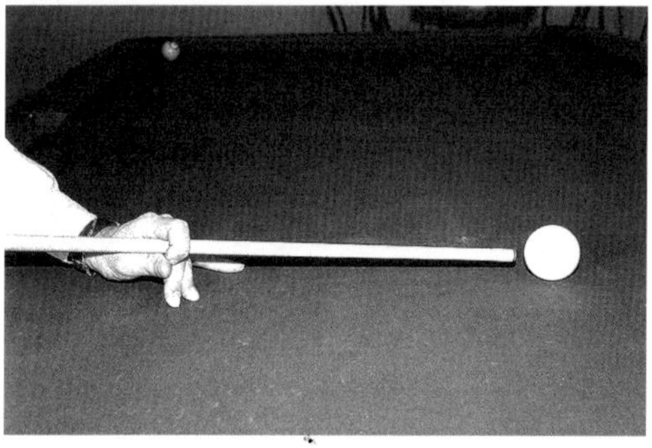

Diagram 99: very long bridge

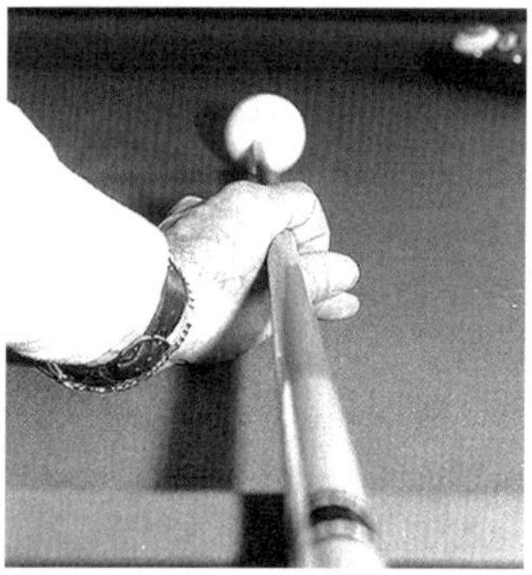

Diagram 100:

On the other hand as seen in example 99 and 100, using a longer bridge the cue ball can be easily viewed and the added few inches here, is good for breaking, however bridging the warm-up strokes into the follow-through requires a highly developed technique as the circle of error here is great. If the straight-through delivery waivers anywhere up to a centimeter in the rear, you run the risk of moving up a half a leather tip diameter and more from the original point of contact on the cue ball.

2.2.2 The stroking hand

The stroking hand is that part of you which executes the actual shot and is therefore responsible for every thing that goes right or wrong in the end. If you are not gripping the cue properly to begin with, you will miss often. We explained earlier "where" to grip the cue, now we will attempt to explain the "how". As the saying goes, "we hope this will help you get a grip on your game".

during ball contact — *during the backswing*

Viewed from the rear — *Viewed from the side*

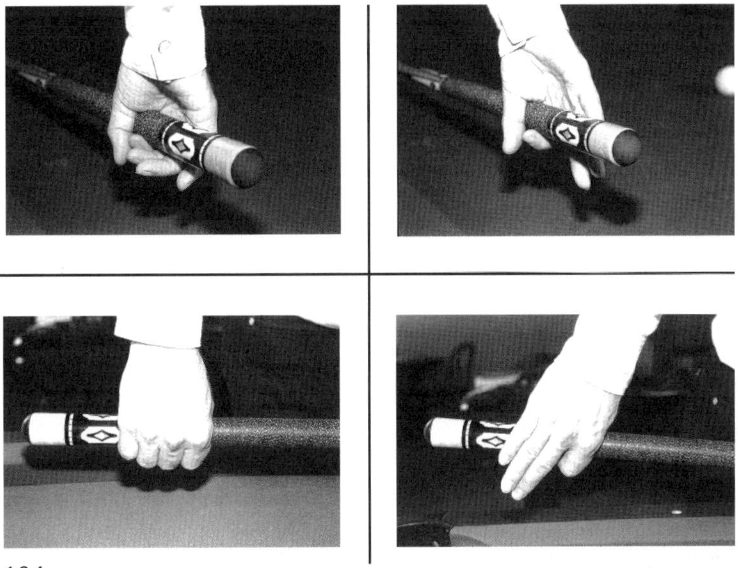

Diagram 101-104

The stroking hand holds the cue just firmly enough, to keep the cue from being dropped in any position you hold it. During aim, the rest of your fingers should grace rather than influence the cues' line of movement, the wrist action during follow-through should happen naturally. (See examples 101 - 104)

Gracefully closing the grip "lightly" as you move the cue forward, offers you the security you may wish in keeping the cue from slipping out of your hand entirely, after a strong follow-through stroke.

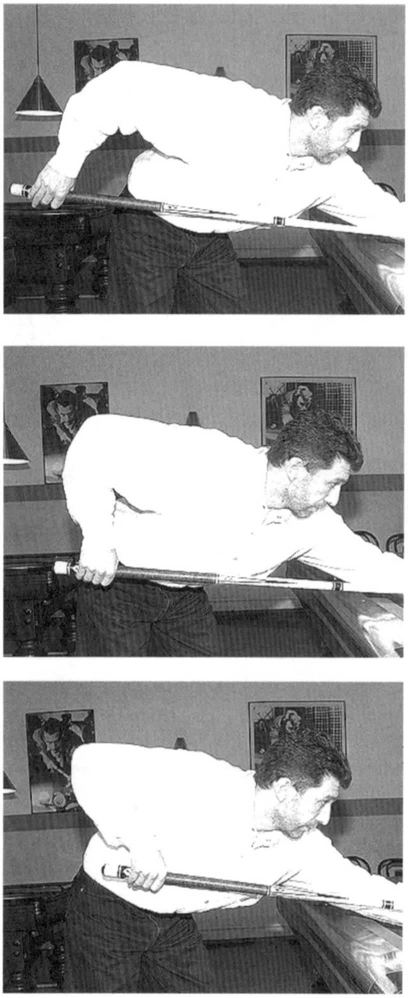

Diagram 105-107

Clenching the cue with a full grip or laying the thumb along the top of the cue will block the fluid wrist action to the rear and can gravely deform your line of aim. If this is forced, the cue shaft can also begin to bounce senselessly up and down on the bridge hand (circle of error). To keep this from happening, never lay your thumb on top of the cue and loosen your grip to a minimum, especially at that point where the cue meets the cue ball, always guide your intentions... don't force them. Even during the break shot, where the grip tends to tighten, the stroking hand should not apply any more tension needed to keep the cue from slipping to the rear or in supporting its forward acceleration. When the leather cue tip is accelerated through the cue ball, the stroking hand should relax somewhat to keep from choking the "energy transfer" to the cue ball. This technique requires practice in the art of "timing". A typical failure during the break shot is that the stroking hand wants to grip the cue tightly, try not to do this. An absolutely pure "energy transfer" during any shot situation, instills insight and understanding in the action you have applied, because the stroke is flowing and the view is undisturbed, which thereby accelerates the learning process and/or solidifies basic beliefs. A good tip for beginners who are comfortable with an open bridge is to practice shooting the cue ball down the length of the table and back at speeds medium and hard. While controlling the distance and direction, see to it that the shaft never leaves your bridge hand during and after the follow-through.

2.2.3 Playing from the rail

All pros use an open bridge off the rail for an undisturbed view.

Diagram 108

If you continue to apply the typical "closed bridge" technique used for the middle of the table, a few problems will accompany you. (See example 108)

Because of one extra factor, you will need to deal with four additional cautions. Factor: One is normally provoked to raise the butt of the cue to hit more of the cue ball. Additional cautions:

- You are unable, to get low enough, to aim properly, especially during long shots.
- If you hit the cue ball hard, it will bounce up.
- If you hit the cue ball outside of its center axis, it will curve away.
- Raising the butt of the cue lowers your accuracy and is therefore uncomfortable.

2.2.3.1 Cue ball is situated on or near the rail.

For normal or standard situations, the following examples show open and closed bridges that are stabile, more effective and therefore well recommended.

Diagram 109; Best for shots between 0-4 inches away Diagram 110-111; Best for shots between 4-12 inches away.

Stance and grip

2.2.3.2 Shooting the cue ball directly from the rail

Shooting from this position is nobody's favorite, while much less than a quarter of the cue ball can be easily influenced. The safest action one can apply here is straight follow. To prevent miscuing, it may help to hold the butt of the cue a little higher than normal, this would be an ideal moment to reassure yourself that your cue tip is properly groomed beforehand, in other words "chalk up"! For this shot the following examples, 112 to 113 are recommended.

Diagram 112

Diagram 113

2.2.3.3 Shooting along the rail

Bridging to shoot the cue ball along the rail may encourage you to use one of the following closed bridges.

Diagram 114-116

2.2.4 Shooting over one or more balls

Here you are encouraged to utilize the open bridge exclusively.

Diagram 117-119

2.2.5 Use of the mechanical bridge

When using the mechanical bridge, the elbow is parallel with the stroking hand as seen in example 120. As you grip the butt of the cue, the cue should rest on the thumb, whereas the rest of your fingers keep the cue from falling. Grasp and stroke the cue as relaxed as otherwise. If any constriction in the gripping is allowed here, the cue will drift to the left or the right, depending on which hand you normally play with and render unwanted English or cause you to miss the shot unless this is expected (see example 121 & 122). The bridge hand should lie on top of the end of the mechanical bridge as seen in example 123. It is often required of the player, directly after shooting, to lift the

Diagram 120: Use of the mechanical bridge

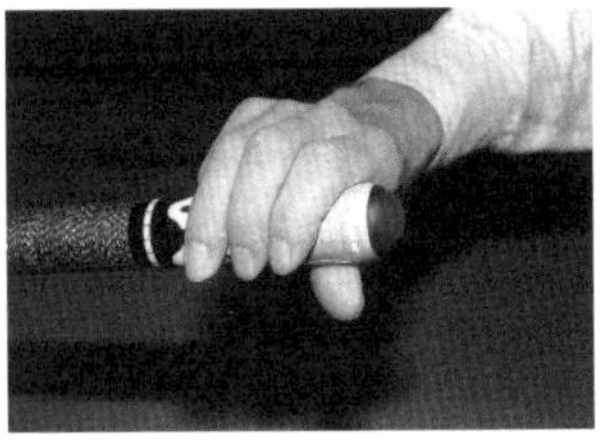

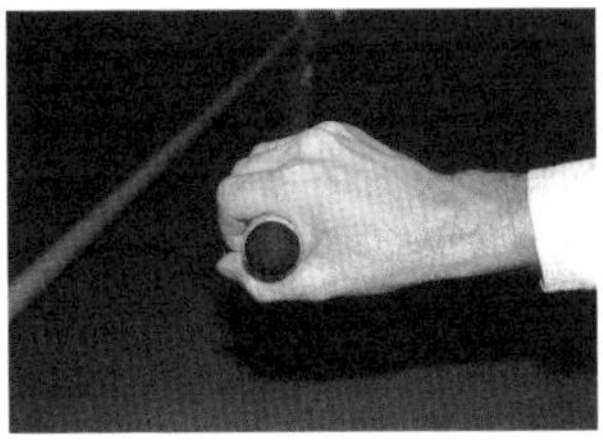

Diagram 121-122

mechanical bridge out of the way of other rebounding balls or the cue ball itself. It is considered foul to impede moving ball progress with a foreign object other than through the natural course of other balls or the rail system itself. Unless you wish to become ambidextrous at this point, you will need to spend a good amount of time of devoted practice in order to master the stroking technique required for the mechanical bridge. The rule of thumb for training lays around 5-10% for beginners.

Diagram 123

Notice:

3. Systematic training concepts

The opinion of eight out of ten average players to the reason for their sometimes bad playing periods is said to come from the lack of concentration. This may be true up to a point, but only when you know what you needed to do beforehand. When questioned how they came to this reasoning, their answer showed only shrugged shoulders. More than half of those players with many years of experience, believe that the reason for their poor ability came from the lack of refined technique. However, to satisfy the question, how this dilemma could be settled at best, was naturally left open.

True, the biggest problem with beginners and hobby players alike is from bad or improper technique. However, the excuse that "one isn't concentrated" is very rarely the reason for a missed ball or not getting "shape" for the next ball. Failure, frustration and loss of motivation are more likely the reason for bringing on the lack of concentration, but only because there is nothing the beginner has understood about their technique that could have helped them make a ball or get shape with certainty. The "mechanics" of technique must be learned! They need to be understood and put to use by design. The mechanics of technique can be "felt", seen" and

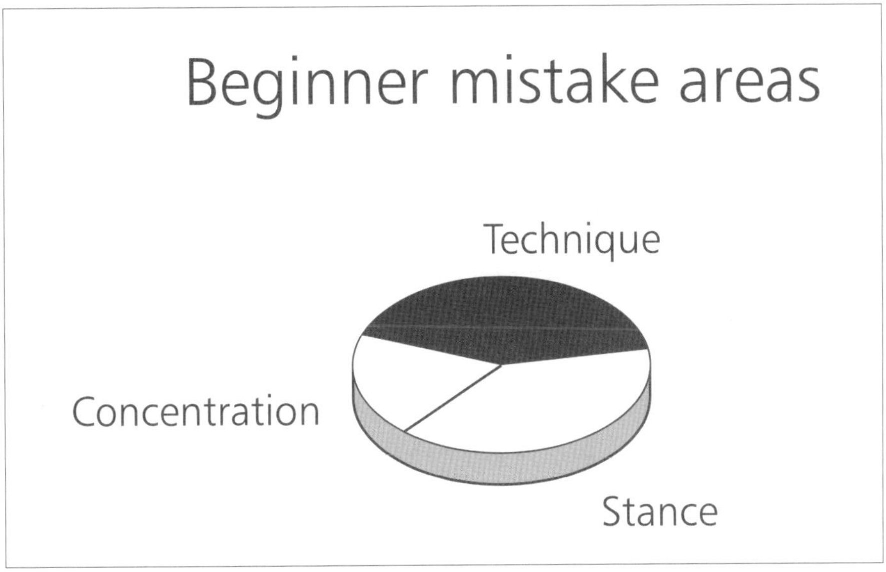

Diagram 124

"followed". This means knowing what needs to be done and concentrating on the learned mechanics of technique with great trust and follow through with them. Gathering knowledge about this game is easy, putting this knowledge to good use by practicing "all the little things" you have learned, to the point where they are a part of you, belongs to the mechanics of your technique. Learning this is the hardest part, especially if you are doing this alone with only this book. All the books, tapes, videos etc. that you may devour on this subject is only 10% of a good lesson and for this reason, nothing compares to a good instructor. However, in order to find the answer still, you must dig a little bit deeper in the world of "technique" with consequence and discipline. Technique is not only a good foundation "why" something you want to perform in the game works the way you wanted it to, it also supports progressive ideas that make mastering new and/or difficult situations possible and builds up confidence. The difference between something that is seldom successful and something that is always successful is the same as the difference between luck and skill. Making a lucky shot or getting "lucky" during a game certainly can make the difference whether you "can" win, or not. The question arises, "do you feel a deserving desire to capitalize on your good fortune or not?" Looking at this in retrospect, how often does one need such luck, to make a shot? To win a game? To win a tournament? Everybody gets lucky now and then, but technique shows skill, not luck. This helps you retain a deserving desire to capitalize on any "good fortune" you may have acquired during this time frame.

When someone wants to better his or her skill at something familiar or new, the basics of the subject matter should be conformed to, refined and polished, before further development can be supported. You should be motivated to work on the mechanics of your technique with more awareness. Just how important this basic form of knowledge is, is explained in the following four diagrams. For beginners, this is the best way to develop an ideal learning program.

Just how important this elemental form of knowledge is, is explained in the following four diagrams. For beginners is this best way to develop an ideal learning program.

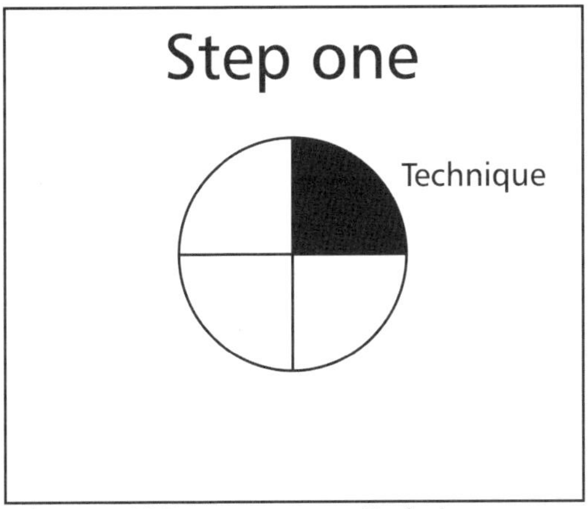

Diagram 125: 1st quarter – Technique

In the first quarter of the learning program, the player should work very intense on their technique, where the grip and stance development lays the utmost importance. The more sensible the basic foundation for the technique is built from, the fewer "bad habits" one needs to master and the faster one learns.

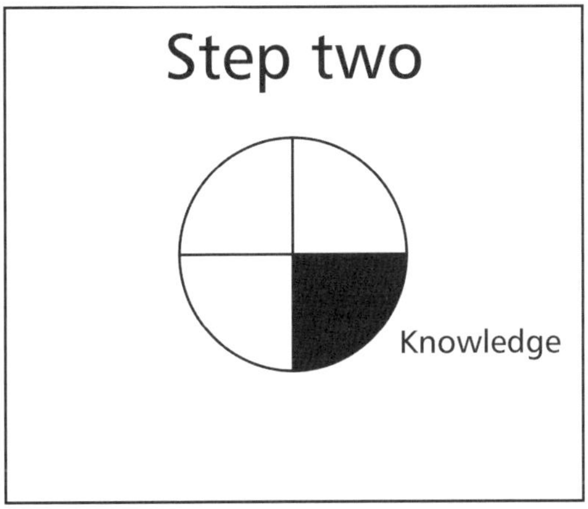

Diagram 126: 2nd quarter – Knowledge

After a good, reproducible technique has been accomplished and you understand how it works (the mechanics), theoretical knowledge becomes increasingly interesting. Stop shot, draw, follow, position play, English and so on. Experiment with these while constantly retaining and refining a good reproducible technique.

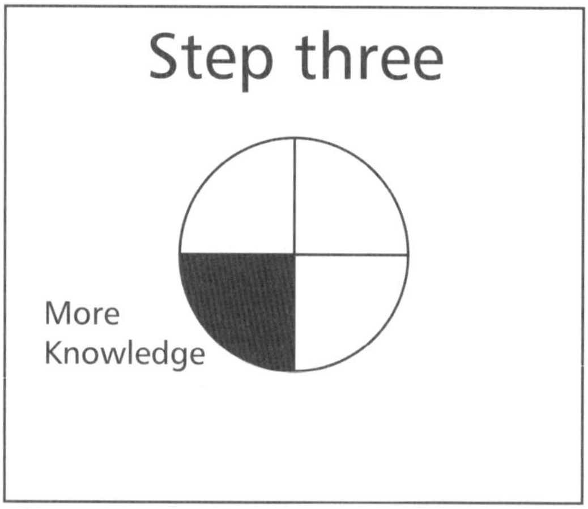

Diagram 127: 3rd quarter – more Knowledge

During the third quarter of the learning program, we are learning knowledge that is more theoretical. Such as: tactics in different disciplines, safety play, and the rail system, special strokes and so on. None of this can help you however, unless the reliance upon the first quarter of the learning program is sound, can be done repeatedly and properly.

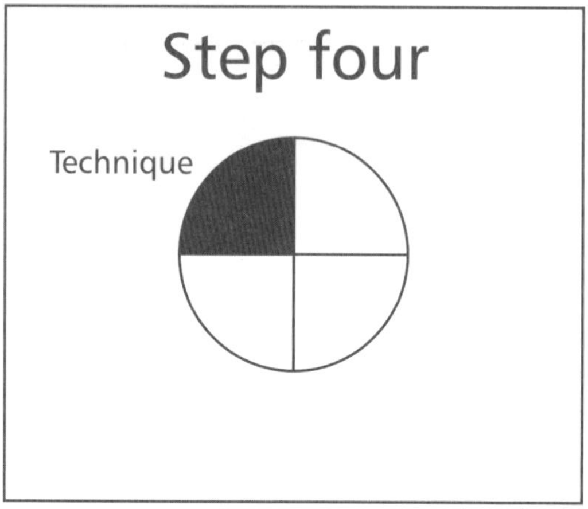

Diagram 128: 4th quarter – Technique

In the fourth quarter, after the student has acquired almost all theoretical knowledge, he returns to the beginning: He refines his technique because, fine tuning his physical coordination will invariably allow him to exceed to the next higher level of play. Most of his faults will be generated from faulty technique, rarely from the lack of knowledge.

Most students, who attend our courses, are players of the 3rd quarter category and were unaware of the importance in the 1st and 4th quarters. Always wanting and becoming more „theoretical knowledge" but lacking the technique to take advantage of it.

3.1 Building blocks for systematic play

Two things you will need to know:

1. First and foremost, you will need to develop your aiming technique. Developing the trust, that what you want to do will happen.
2. Second, after the warm-up, the follow-through stroke is refined, fluid, straight and ends 8 to 12 cm past that point where the cue ball was laying and is the perfectly understood and aligned extension to step one.

If these two steps are not performed perfectly, your final expectations should not be very high. For example, Always making the shot and getting expected shape for the next.

Separating these two steps (aiming and follow-through stroke) is a very important aspect for obtaining good technique in a player. Aiming is of course important, but not as important as the follow-through stroke. Aiming will come to you if you understand your delivery and follow it first. The reason for this is that a faulty follow-through stroke-in the long run-causes the player more problems than incorrect aiming. Getting "ready" for something is the first important step in simplifying the most difficult situations and therefore, understanding how your follow-through stroke works in the end and getting ready for it, should dominate how you aim the shot. Many players think just the opposite and most would tend to believe that both aspects are equally important, but the fact of the matter is, most missed shots during big tournaments are exclusively due to not concentrating enough on the outcome or not being completely convinced as to how the cue ball is going to react to their follow-through stroke.

3.1.1 Follow through technique

Let us start with an allegation, that for many may seem paradox and/ or surprising:

"No professional will ever be able to control the cue ball and/or object ball completely".

We would wager, that the balloon for "high expectations" in a beginner has just been popped... One might think that pros may even go on the offensive, by saying, "You surely can't mean me?" Many students in our course, having heard this claim for the first time, would chuckle at first. Some would even go so far as to ask, what they should expect to learn from this course in the end, if not that?

True, such a statement is not very motivating for one who expects to learn this sport completely. However, the fact of the matter is, this is the "big secret" all good players wish to relate to all their opponents. When you have completed the readings in chapter three, come back to our above claim and check its credibility. If you then find this statement to be a true, you will then realize what it is you *really* need to work on.

3.1.1.1 Control

Let us take the above statement and analyze the word that upset us the most: (Control) this is a very strong word, especially when one can only do other things in life, simply correct! Look at the difference in the definition between "correct" and "control" and decide which definition comes closer to "exactness", naturally the word control.

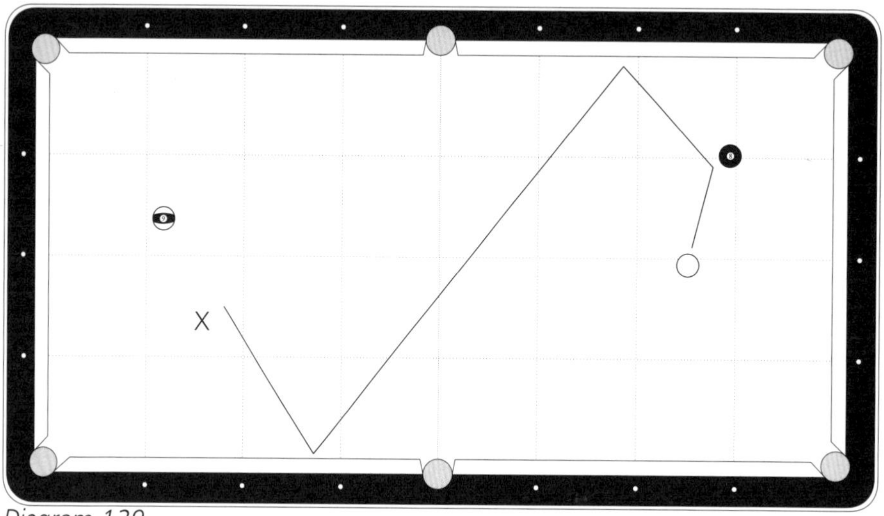

Diagram 129

To have "control" over a situation is one thing, to have control over movement is another. Only machines can control movement close enough to exactness, where the naked eye cannot see the difference and the occurrence created or set into motion is executed the exact same way every time.

Reproducible exactness means controlled occurrences and if this where possible in pool then the sport would loose its attractiveness. We hope that the following example will broaden your insight as to how position play is ordinarily focused upon.

In the above example, our player has achieved position on the 9-ball right where "X" marks the spot. Good, no big problem for him but lets set the situation up again. Question: what are the odds that the cue ball will find its way, exactly where "X" marks the spot, a second time? Rather than dwelling on this question in its simple form, let us consider for a moment, the effort that is needed to reproduce this outcome perfectly. You will need to hit the shot with the exact same speed. The cue ball and object ball must touch at the exact same angle and the cue tip must drive through the face of the cue ball at the exact same point and manner.

Three objectives must be achieved perfectly:

- Follow-through speed.
- Point of hit between cue ball and object ball.
- Point of hit and manner with the cue tip on the cue ball.

Therefore, if these three objectives were orchestrated perfectly a second time, one would achieve an absolute identical occurrence. If only one of these objectives (meaning; only one) were changed, however slightly, one would consequently receive another, perhaps similar occurrence. Changing the speed of the follow-through stroke will cause the cue ball to come up short or roll past the mark. A different reaction will occur if only the object ball is hit thinner or thicker "or" if the cue tip strikes the face of the cue ball in anything other than the original manner. Any of these changes done individually, where the other two are performed perfectly, will invariably cause different reactions in the cue balls final position. If however, you were to change two or all three of these parameters, it is quite possible for the cue ball to still land on the "X" a second time. For example, a thinner hit on the eight ball but more left English or draw may still bring the cue ball back on the mark. Onlookers would either consider this a tremendous show of skill or an unbelievable amount of luck and unless you are quite famous, the latter would apply.

Going back to our simple question, what the odds are in doing this a second time? We invite you to try this 10 times. Either by moistening the finger tip to mark the end position or marking this clearly with a piece of chalk. Any professional "shooting from the hip" could present us with the above example.

Systematic training concepts

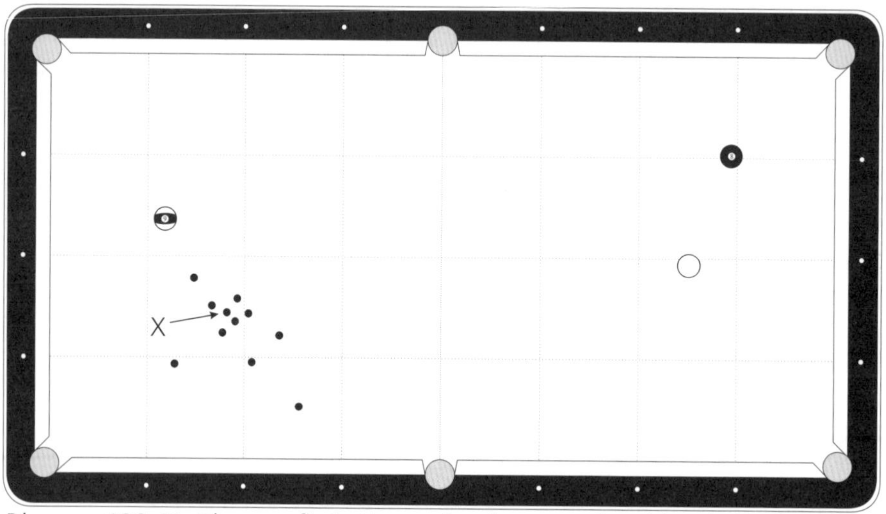

Diagram 130: X=The very first attempt for shape on the object ball, after which ten attempts were tried to reach the first.

The area an experienced player will require is normally greater and of course the position points a beginner will generate, range from 50 to 100 percent of the surface area available. Incidentally, watch out for the side pocket closest to you.

When you complete this, analyze your level of play, using the following Grading System.

- Maximum of three times in ten attempts, the cue ball lands in the area of one sq meter: Read the next chapter thoroughly, it will help you greatly.
- Maximum of five times in ten attempts, the cue ball lands in the area of one sq meter: For the "hobby or past time player, this is an enormous accomplishment! If the same however,

wishes to win tournaments with a spread as broad as this, they are not being very realistic. The system in your game here is too inconsistent.

- Maximum of seven times in ten attempts, the cue ball lands in the area, half of that required in the above requirements: Good, but although your game system shows very good traits, you still have much room for improvements.
- Seven out of ten attempts, the cue ball lands in the area of a page out of a college notebook: Very good, you know what it takes for a good reproducible game system and conquer many challenges required.
- Eight out of ten attempts, the cue ball lands in the area of a page out of a college notebook: Outstanding! If you can do this all the time, you have a reproducible game system and can join the ranks of the best players in the game. Congratulations, we do not guess your reading this book to learn anything and we expect you will be participating in the next world championship.

Fact is, the best players in the world will find this target area quite normal but to be able to hit their original mark a second time in ten attempts, may very well cost them a gray hair or two. This target area is a

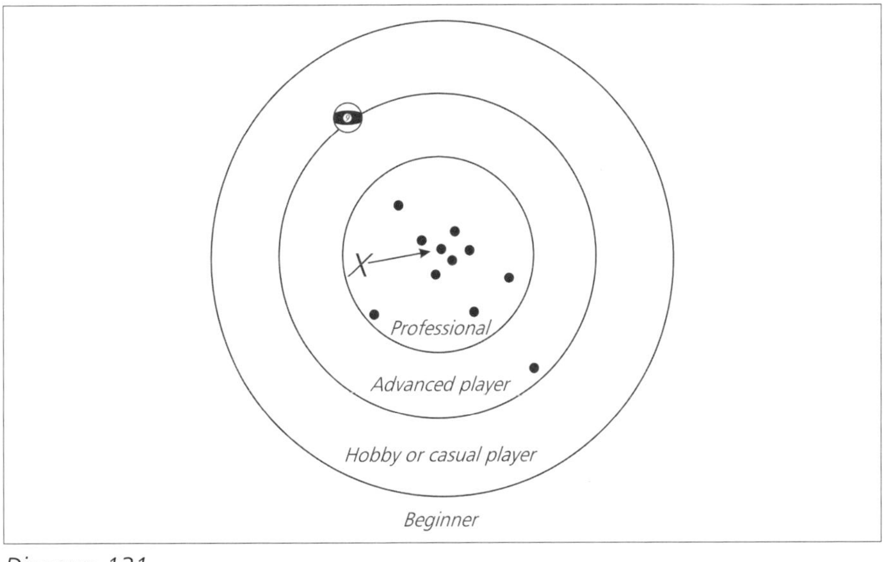

Diagram 131

guideline on just how good a player is, then a rule of thumb is: The smaller the "spread" the better the player.

The smaller the „spread" the better the player is.

Of course, there are game situations that are easy to duplicate. One thinks about "stop shots" that are two feet away or small distance draws. This can be done by pros and advanced players ten out of ten times. However, perfectly tailored situations where all is needed is small draws, follow, or stop shots is not a realistic way of looking at this sport and should not be considered as complete control of the balls. After making the shot, getting "snow" to move to an "area of attack" for the next shot is usually required, and your not always going to find this easy. Further more, getting "very good" at the above situation may not mean that you can join the ranks of the best players in the world, but it will definitely make it clear, how good your control needs to be to get there.

Systematic training concepts

When we talk about control in pool (this goes for all other sport disciplines as well) we mean that reproducible control that we can produce continuously and similar.

What is it really, that the player "actually" controls? What is it that makes the players ability constant? You should know that it is not the balls and it is certainly not the table. However, the answer to this question is certainly "at hand". The cue!

Diagram 132

Leading the cue in the same, coordinated manner allows for similar and understandable occurrences during play. The difference in ability between Pro amateurs on up and many experienced players on down is that many experienced players have spent their entire life trying to control the balls. Whereas pros have learned long ago, it is the cue that they really need to control. No professional would ever blame the balls or the way they act entirely. How the balls can react is a direct result of your knowledge and coordination with the cue itself.

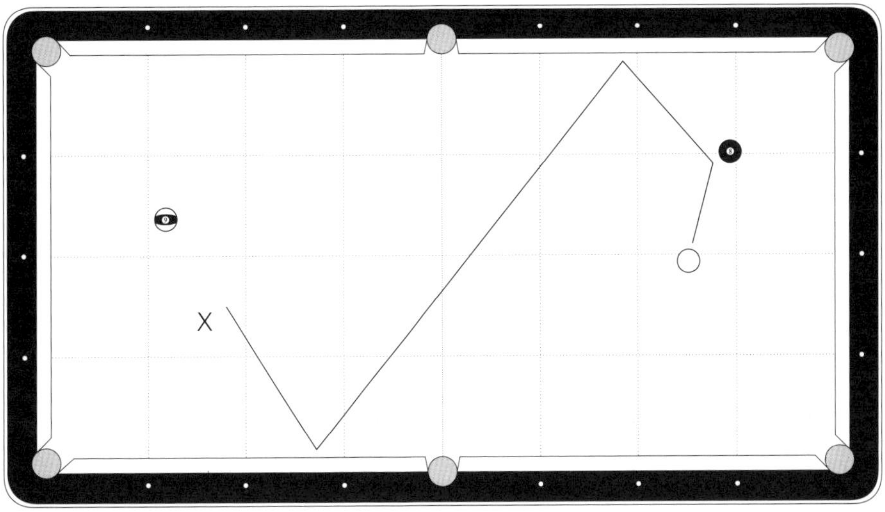

Diagram 134

However, to get back to our above example, the spread shows that pinpoint positioning is not all that important to a professional. The real importance here lies in getting within range of the next objective with the correct angle (shape) that allows them to move to the next target area correctly with the cue ball. Generating the energy required in the cue ball to move from one shape area to the next on the pool table, or from one easy shot to the next, allows the pro to pace his concentration. This will invariably leave him enough reserve to get out of tight situations when they come up.

It will take a beginner many years to understand how to do everything the pro is able to do on a pool table as controlled and as "seemingly" perfect as the professional can, but getting there is half the fun. As beginners grow to be professionals, there shape area becomes more defined and smaller. Trail and error through proper training has taught them how to look for the best possibilities and their feel for the game is much more refined. Our second book on this subject, will give you more insight at getting and seeing the best possible position or shape areas. It will also help you understand the environment you are dealing with, namely the table and its pockets.

3.1.1.2 The follow-through stroke

What is "a good stroke?" For that matter, "what is a good follow-through stroke and what are its characteristics?"

Given the fact, that regular players of the game, have shot the cue ball well over a thousand times, most of them cannot easily give you a clear definition. This question may even be difficult for a pro to answer, whereas pros are excused. They at least know what they are doing and how to do it again. To give it a name, must have lost its immediate interest quite a few years ago.

Jerry Briesath queried us future trainers with the above questions and to date, we were quite astounded as to how unable we were, to give him a concrete answer. Given our intentions for attending and completing this course and what we have accomplished thus far, looking back, this was an important question! Let us begin the answer to this question with a little "mind game".

While watching a much better player than yourself, have you ever said to yourself; "How could I ever be able to beat this guy?" He worked his way around the table, executing shots with impressive authority, didn't he? No question, this was a good player, but let us take this experiment one step further.

Imagine yourself observing a match between two persons, who are unknown to you, in some tournament, somewhere. Little do you know, one is a seasoned professional, the other is an absolute beginner. However, you are unable to determine this as both have nice cues and are wearing tuxedos to begin with. However, at that point in the match, where both players had a chance to deal with their individual situations for the first time, you knew which player you would lay your money on (the hard part here maybe, is finding someone to take you up on it!). During the match, you quickly realize which player is more comfortable at the table.

What was it about these two players that allowed you to be certain, practically from the beginning, which player was better? The one had something he could relay on that the other could not, right? A good solid reason that you used to pick out your winner was crystallized in the authority they each applied to the cue ball and the outcome of their decisions. In the better of the two, you may have noticed, he would normally hit the ball the same way every time and while observing the response after his deliverance, would rarely move his cue immediately. Taking the term "deliverance" and renaming it "the follow-through stroke", what is a good stroke? In addition, which characteristics should be listed in its definition?

Simply defined:

Follow-through stroke: A straight forward throwing movement, generated gradually to the cue ball, after which the cue tip comes to rest roughly 10 cm past that place where the cue ball was laying.

We will take this definition and break it down even further:

- straight forward
- throwing movement
- generated gradually
- roughly 10 cm past
- cue tip comes to rest

3.1.1.3 straight forward

Simply said but not easily done. Nonetheless, this is by far the most important aspect for continued success in billiards. Not giving your follow-through stroke this due amount of attention, will consequently cost you either a missed shot or bad shape. The harder you hit, the harder it is to keep the cue straight.

A follow-through stroke that is not always straight when it needs to be, gives the player his highest form of insecurity. This can come from an incorrect stance, improper state of readiness (chin-log), other things or possibilities are being thought about during the stroke, cramped stroking over other balls, pocket, etc., etc.

Another reason for a faulty alignment into the follow-through stroke could come from inconsistent or improper aiming techniques. By this we mean, shooting the ball before knowing for certain that the line of aim is correct. For example: The player leaned around into the shot (felt "chin-log" was unimportant, left out commonly when the shot is hard or is

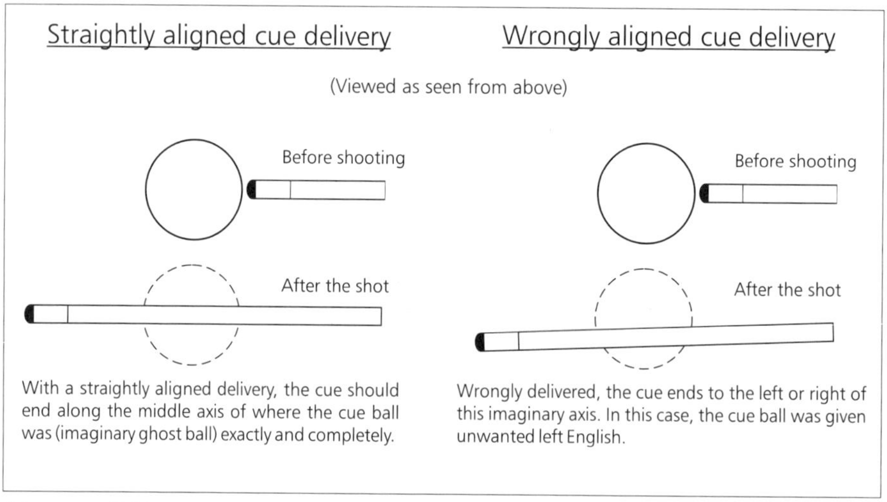

Diagram 135:

unaware of this technique) and during his warm-up stroke is unsure of his alignment before completing the follow-through stroke, but thinks he can blindly feel the shot in somehow and shoots anyway.

After which, the player realizes he hit the cue ball naturally there where he feared he shouldn't and attempts to correct this too late. This type of deliverance known as body language or jerking is apparent in young as well as experienced players, but has absolute no effect on the outcome of the shot itself. Given the experience level of a player, who is under heavy pressure in a match and nervous, this show of over reaction can begin, sadly enough, during the hitting phase of the follow-through stroke. Few of them are aware that this is an instinctive reaction, coming from the sudden realization of what is going to happen against for what was hoped. Stop hoping for better play, work for it! Let your Mother, Friends or others close to you, hope for you. To play better, eventually you need to know what is going to happen always... To begin to understand this better, you need of course to practice on the Mechanics of your Technique, but before this can be of help, we need to explain the problems you can run into.

For the beginner, finding the alignment (or noticing the lack of it) into the follow-through stroke may be quite difficult to see, not to mention hard to correct in the beginning when discovered. Never the less, help on how to refine this, will be explained. Given a limited target surface on the cue ball, which is roughly five cm (minus the 1 cm slip zone on the

Diagram 136: How different players observe striking points on the cue ball

outer ring) there are numerous points of contact that can be applied from the leather tip. For the beginner, the cue ball is simply looked upon as one entire target surface that needs to be directed into another, which hopefully leads an object ball to a pocket. Therefore, those motivated beginners, wanting certain results to happen correctly, must learn to hit the correct point of contact on the cue ball much more asserted and consciously. They should be aware that these various "possible" points of contact, relay various "inevitable" reactions to the cue ball, and is advised in the beginning to exercise strong limits.

Systematic training concepts

While the beginner is wandering through uncharted territory at this stage, the hobby player understands to some extent, how the cue ball reacts to middle axis strokes, i.e.: follow and to some extent stop and draw ball action. English use is also a familiar phrase however, they are much better at speaking it, than using it on the cue ball. On the other hand, experienced players and professionals understand the inevitable reactions in a certain point of contact on the cue ball, (see diagram 136) where the various possible paths for follow or draw are carefully chosen, and taken advantage of. However, in order to understand these inevitable reactions and use them effectively, straightforwardness in the follow-through stroke on the middle axis must be an ability that can be done repeatedly.

Beginners should concentrate primarily on hitting the cue balls middle or perpendicular axis as this offers little consequence for making balls regularly and understandably.

3.1.1.4 throwing movement – generated gradually *(speed)*

A good follow-through stroke is actually a throwing movement, where drawing the cue back slowly (similar to drawing back a bow and arrow or

Diagram 137: Other types of sports which involve throwing movements

winding up to throw a hard ball or the back swing in golf) has its beginning.

The common flaw found here is incorrectly orchestrated technique. As in all sports where precision arm movements are used to initiate desired direction, i.e.: Golf, Billiards, Darts, Baseball, Tennis, Javelin, etc., the back swing has little to no great speed ever. If the golfer on a "driving range" were to swing his club as fast backwards as he would during his follow-through stroke, he would loose all control over his bodily coordination. In this case, because separate muscle groups need to change opposite directions so quickly, he would loose his feel for the original line of aim and probably plow into the ground next to the ball he intended to send to the moon! The upper and lower arm "muscle control", concerning these two opposite directions must be initiated gradually, if a 100% feeling for the original line of aim is to be felt, understood and managed. The follow-through stroke is normally always faster than the back-swing but remember, the faster the follow-through stroke is, the faster and harder you want to grab the cue and therefore the harder it is to throw the cue-stick through the cue-ball straight. You need to learn how to generate the desired speed gradually.

3.1.1.5 roughly 10 cm past

The throwing fluidness the cue-tip has to the cue ball is an important characteristic for a good follow-through stroke. When we talk about "roughly 10 cm past", we mean the cue-tip is a distance between 8 and 12 cm past where the cue ball was laying. This distance will vary from one player to another, because of the length of ones forearm. The important matter here is that you keep the distance past the cue ball constant for all shots where this is possible (We will show two examples where this isn't

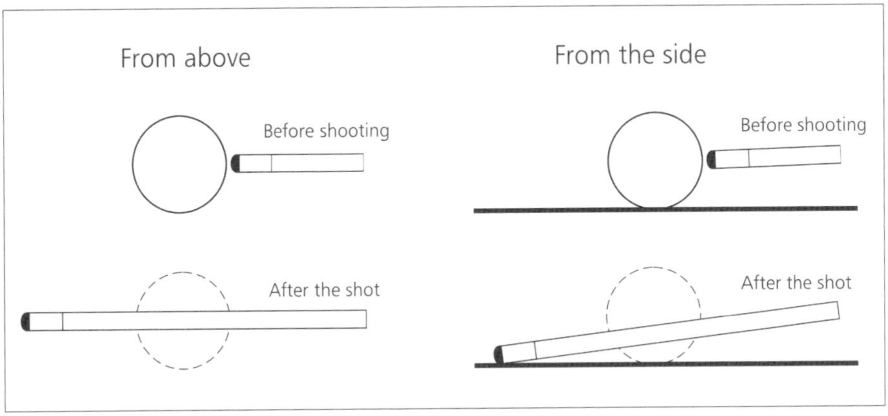

Diagram 138: Following to and through the cue ball as seen from above and from the side.

possible, later). For the beginner, this also belongs to the mechanics of technique and helps you achieve a better feel for cue ball movement.

We define three reasons why this is so important:

- Allowing the cue to travel through the cue ball releases any "will" to hold back the stroke in the beginning. Understanding and trust has a chance to build in you. You begin to relax, yet at the same time consequently play more efficiently and concentrated.
- Building upon constant and controllable factors is the fastest way to learn the mechanics of your technique. A "measured stroke" is constant and controllable, therefore understandable, easy to remember and more important you can do it repeatedly. Holding back or "jerking" propels the cue ball to the object ball in a manner that you can only hope for and never be able to consistently reproduce.
- In doing so, the tip contact on the cue ball is more exact and greatly reduces the diameter of your "circle of error" (see: the cue comes to rest). A smoothly delivered stroke is the difference between getting the cue ball to draw back to you as wished or through "jerking" only receiving a stop shot.

The psychological aspect here, without going in too deep: Through a consequent follow-through, to and through where the cue ball was laying, one directs the game away from oneself.

Beginners as well as many amateurs holdup their stroke or "jerk", right after the hit on the cue ball is made, due to fear that the cue may touch the cue ball a second time. A prime example here is the expectations after a closely situated draw shot.

We mentioned earlier that there are two exceptions to the rule here:

1. When breaking the rack open with a high amount of energy, professionals want to get the cue ball speed up. The distance between the chin and cue is often much greater, the bridge is longer and they hold the cue further back. This enables them to drive the cue much further than 12 cm through the cue ball. One might observe that some move their entire body for a short distance forward and their elbow drops to the cue to keep the cue level and get the maximum distance possible through the cue ball. Whether this is good or not, the professional up to this point has won a great deal of matches and has therefore a great deal of experience

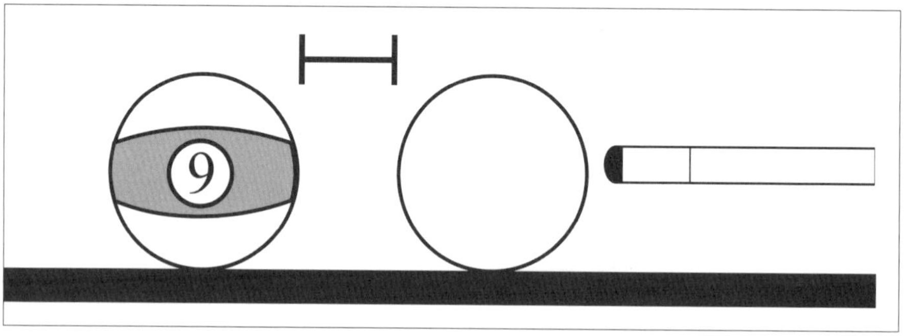

Diagram 139: The cue ball is too close

with his break. We refrain from advising a beginner to follow such an example, as the control over the cue ball is practically impossible for the beginner to contain.

2. In diagram 139, stroking through the cue ball 8-12 cm would certainly cause the cue tip to "re-hit" the cue ball a second time. This of

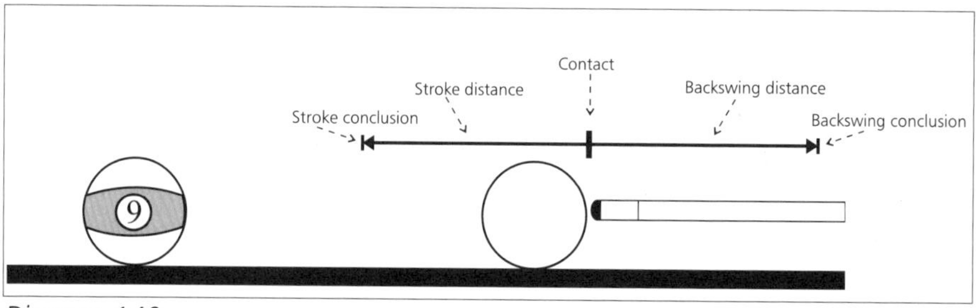

Diagram 140

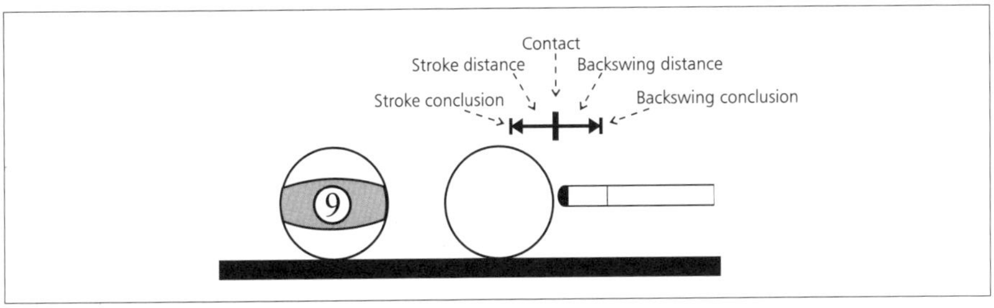

Diagram 141

course, is a foul, to which your opponent can normally see. Therefore, the follow-through must be shortened. When the cue ball is under 8-12 cm from the object ball, the back swing should show the distance of freedom, the cue tip is allowed to travel through the cue ball. (see diagram 141) In this case, the condition should be clear. If one were to draw back 10 cm and wish to stop the cue tip 3 cm after hitting the cue ball, a measured end to the final outcome can only be guessed at (3.1 cm is a foul because you will hit the cue ball twice. Or, stop "too short" and jerk back in fright and you've got to laugh at yourself a little, because you didn't even hit the cue ball). The same principle can be observed by golfers: When the golfer putts he won't draw his putter back as far for a 12 inch putt as he would with his driving iron to reach 200 yards.

Systematic training concepts

3.1.1.6 The cue tip comes to rest

This is the only point of time, where the "Circle of Error" can be noticed and for the beginner the only way one can understand in the follow-through stroke: "what went wrong?" or "what went right?" We either learn to correct this or record this ability in our memory bank and duplicate it the next time. The circle of error as described by Jerry Briesath, is that point struck on the cue ball face with the cue tip that cannot be pinpointed exactly. For example: A pros circle of error for any given shot on the average is 1/20th of an inch, the advanced player 1/8th of an inch, the average player 1/4th of an inch and beginners as described here later, between 1/3rd and the size of a golf ball! It is quite human to "rise up quickly" after a shot is executed, and observe what is happening, many good players and lesser do this regularly, even some pros who are extensively expressive. However, with exception to the professional, all others should first understand where and how their stroke is ending and see to it, that the cue tip is resting exactly where and how you expected.

3.1.1.7 Stabilize the elbow level

Keeping the elbow level stabilized during the warm-up stroke is a trade mark many professionals display. During the follow-through stroke a stabilized elbow level gives the beginner an added advantage. Stabilizing the elbow during the follow-through will make the cue tip dive on or near the table surface, depending on where the cue ball was hit. Few professionals however, will execute a follow shot in this manner but never the

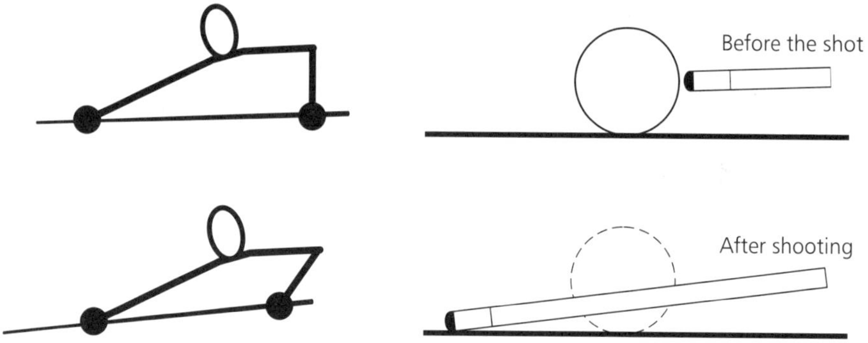

Diagram 142: Stroke delivery while stabilizing the elbow and upper arm.

less the tip may sometimes, still move in the direction of the table surface. The examples demonstrated in 142-147 show three different cue ball hit levels (draw, stop and follow) where the elbow level is stabilized.

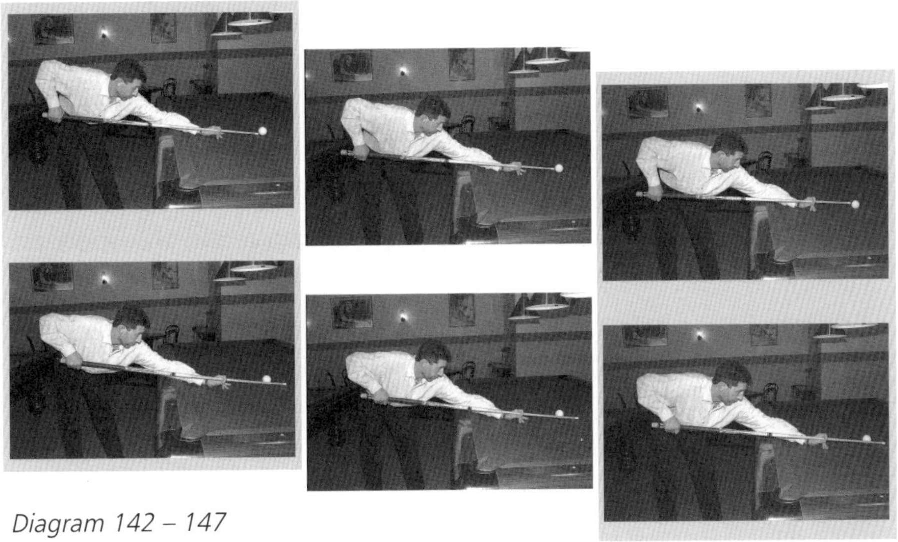

Diagram 142 – 147

There are two common flaws related to this delivery, which need to be emphasized.

- The elbow moves up and down during the warm-up stroke and drops further during the follow-through (inexperienced players).
- Only during the follow-through stroke does the elbow drop (experienced players).

Hitting the desired point on the cue ball for the expected direction and action needed, can not be accomplished regularly if the cue tip is being whipped or waved into the delivery point on the cue ball (another factor belonging to the Circle of Error). When the elbow is moving up and down, the wave sequence is exceedingly quick and flat, making it impossible to know whether the cue tip is on the way up to the delivery point or on the way down. Therefore, this gives one only a 50:50 chance (max!) of an expected outcome. Not very good odds for a reproducible technique.

We emphasize good reasons for stabilizing the elbow once more:

- The point of contact on the cue ball and the manner in which it should be hit is more exact.
- The distance traveled through where the cue ball was laying, is constant.

Consistency in the delivery is of the utmost importance for reproducible success, because the innumerous factors involved in this sport are controllable only if the technique is simplified and consequently followed.

Letting the elbow sink during the follow-through allows the tip to rise above the original or desired striking point on the cue ball surface. This technique is full of innumerous factors, because the further up on the cue ball struck, can create a different and often unwanted cue ball reaction. Stabilize that elbow and you create a constant basic factor that is better understood and foreseeable.

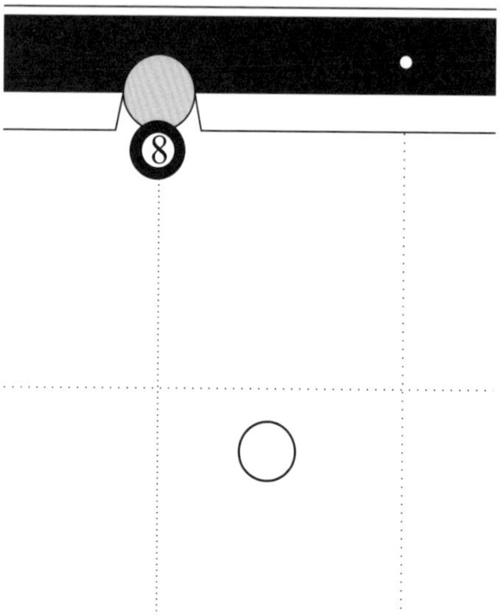

Diagram 148: The following game situation is a typical hurdle that most beginners and novice players have big problems with.

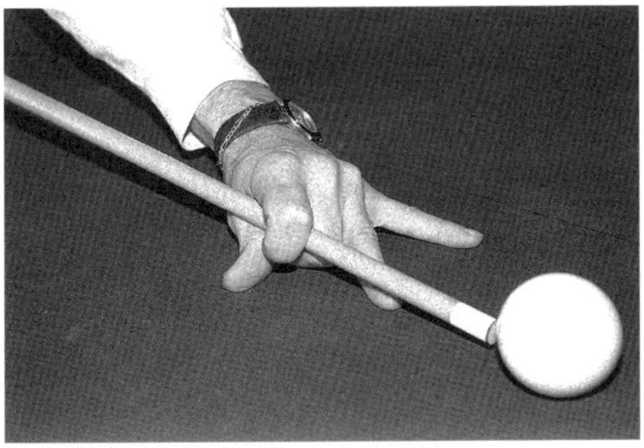

Diagram 149

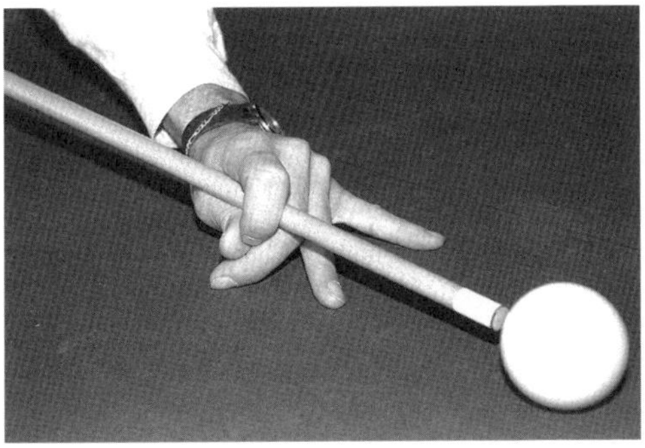

Diagram 150

The objective here is to simply draw the cue ball. Young players know from watching and observing others, that the cue ball must be hit low. However, when they try this shot, they often drop their elbow before the cue tip reaches the cue ball. When the elbow drops before hitting the cue ball, you invariably touch the cue ball surface above the intended striking point.

"Uh oh, that didn't work!" Is the first thing you might have said to yourself, right? O.K., well what did you do the next time? Beginners and novice players, lacking the supervision of an experienced trainer or player, will invariably think that the lack of power is the reason for not achieving a good draw ball. Watch out here! Bad habits are hard to break and means they just drop their elbow faster! Nothing is less calculable, than uncontrolled energy explosions and even less understood even less. The more you follow the mechanics of your technique, the faster you can develop, so begin by stabilizing your elbow.

3.1.2 Aiming techniques

There are many "aiming techniques". However, when aiming directly at the object ball with the cue ball, there are two basic systems.

- The point system
- The ghost-ball system

Many players have decided on either one or the other. However, there are those who find it more effective to use both.

3.1.2.1 The point system

Many players, either consciously or unconsciously of the fact, use the point system method. Where two important points of reference for the cue ball to the object ball are recognized and aimed at:

- The touching point.
- The aiming point.

The "touching point" (see diagram) is the next point opposite the initial direction on the object ball and exactly half a ball in height. It is

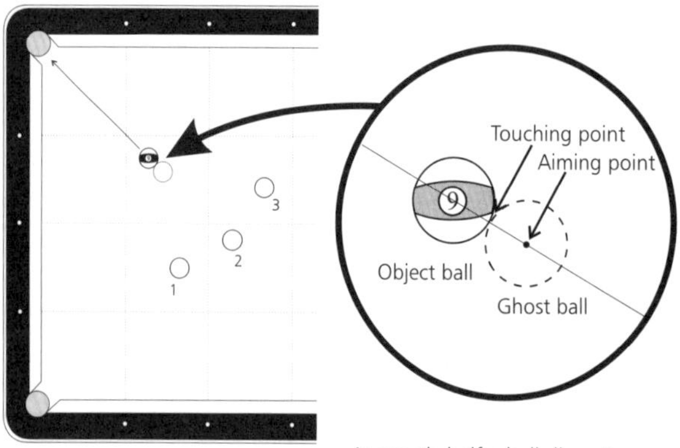

Diagram 151

At exactly half a ball diameter...
... Lays the aiming point and the touching point from one another
... Lays the touching point on the object ball above the table surface.

obvious, that the touching point on the cue ball is therefore opposite that of the object ball during contact, only that the cue ball comes, exactly a half ball in height and depending on the situation, from different angles.

The aiming point however, is exactly a half ball away from the touching point on the object ball. On the cue ball, this aim should be at its middle. When these two aiming points pass through exactly, the touching points on both object and cue ball meet exactly as well.

3.1.2.2 The ghost ball system

The "ghost-ball system is the simple version of the "point-system" only this system requires more imagination on the part of the player. Fact is, the beginner understands and utilizes this method of aiming better than any other method. This system sticks with many beginners even after they become professionals.

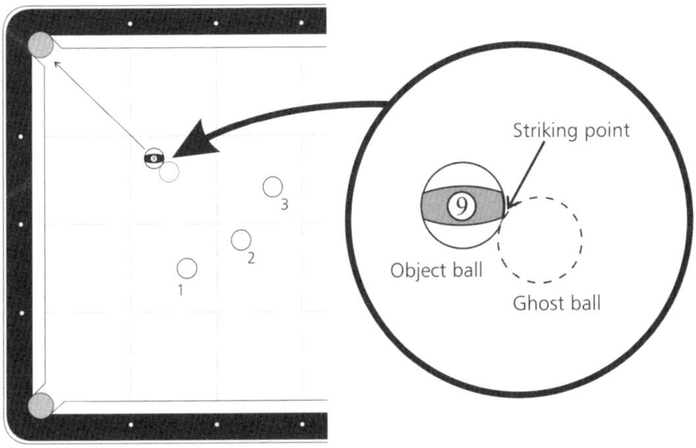

Diagram 152

A bit of trivial information: Not too many years ago in Europe, it was allowed for one to use a free object-ball to express the "ghost-balls" position and to check exactly, whether or not, the cue-ball could pass freely to the intended object-ball without brushing any interference. Because the rules of play are now international, this is of course no longer allowed.

3.1.2.3 Chin lock – where aiming begins

Systematic training concepts

Very often, the reason for missing or not achieving entirely an intended goal, stems from incorrect timing. A good rhythm is unconsciously moved up a notch and the player starts to "lean around" into the line of aim. For example: sliding the hand on the table and leaning around into the line of aim before the aiming eye is online with the cue. Correcting and adjusting while "down on the ball". Often one realizes that their aim is not entirely correct and still chooses to "stay down" while correcting. If your adjustments are within small fractions of an inch, you will unlikely have a serious problem. However, any adjustments close to and over a half inch should move you to "get up" and line the shot up seriously. These adjustments of one, two and more times can be avoided if you position yourself behind the line of aim correctly from the beginning. The visualization of any shot should always take place in your mind first and because your mind is above everything else vital in you physically, you should give it a chance to visualize the aim, namely from above. This "visualization" from above we are describing here is used in all forms of Billiards and may be better known as "Chin lock". The player in this instance draws an imaginary path to his goal with his chin. This helps him to visualize in his mind first, the possible outcome and helps him to "log on" to the correct line of aim. This invariably enables him to see where he needs to "get down" into a correct stance consistently behind the cue ball. Done correctly, a player who understands the mechanic of his technique well, could feasibly, after setting up behind the cue ball and without using warm-up strokes at the aiming point on the object ball, make the object ball with closed eyes or come very close. Try this:

Diagram 153

Set the balls up as in Diagram 154, where the cue ball is on the head spot and the object ball is on the side rail by the second diamond.

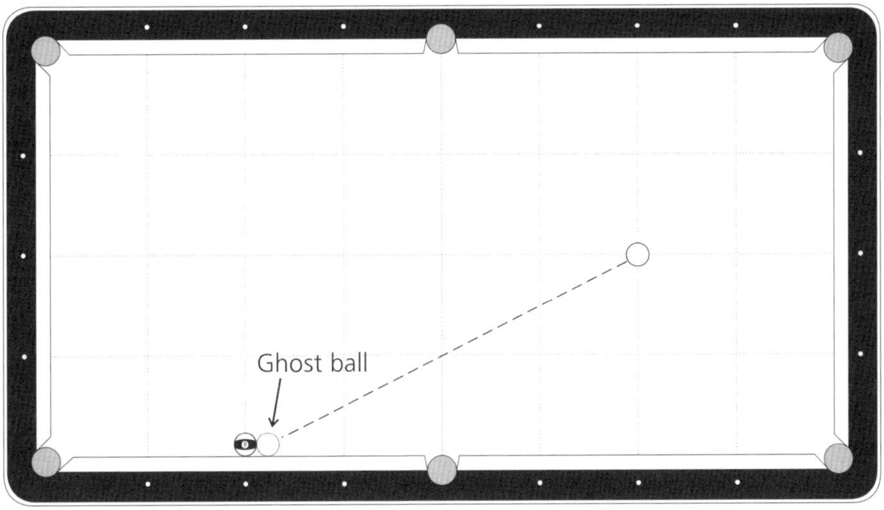

Diagram 154

Utilizing the chin lock technique that we have described here, visualize first your line of aim, to make the object ball in the corner pocket. Aim for a half-ball hit and position yourself behind the line of aim so, that when you move into your stance, you are comfortable at the onset. Visualize what you are about to have happen, a couple of times. Now, concentrating on keeping your chin over the line of aim, move into your stance behind the cue ball until the cue is exactly under the chin and over the line of aim. At this point, the cue tip should be pointing exactly at the middle of the cue ball. Take one warm-up stroke to insure a comfortable delivery and then hold the cue-tip close behind the cue ball. Resist the urge to use your normal warm-up aiming procedure. Close your eyes. Pull the cue back slowly and evenly and follow-through gradually up to medium speed, 8-12 cm past where the cue ball was laying and freeze! Without looking to see if you made the shot or not, look first to where you are holding your line of aim. Be honest with yourself, is the cue directly over the head-spot? If it is, then you have already heard the telltale, satisfying clunk of the object ball falling in the pocket or you at least "rattled it in the jaws"!

Chin lock is the method used by most of the professionals the world over, to automatically find their correct stance. It keeps one normally, from having to make drastic adjustments once the stance has been moved into. Although, chin lock shows the pro where the aim should be, it will not replace correct aiming procedures entirely. It is however, a very helpful tool and builds confidence. Every good player should integrate chin lock in each shot interval, regardless of its simplicity.

3.2 Playing system

Systematic training concepts

As we mentioned earlier, a good playing system is built upon sound technique during the aiming and delivery phase. We have described in detail all of what this entails. Now let us go through the entire aiming, stroking and follow-through phase, systematically touching on those points of interest in quick format.

Think first of an ordinary shot that can be easily foreseeable and mastered. Find the aiming point, the ghost ball or both on the object ball. Stand behind the cue ball with the same foot on the chin lock line of aim the stroking arm is. Log the middle of the cue ball online with the aiming point on the object ball. Let the shot take place in your mind a couple of times and predict in advance how you expect the shot to turn out. Holding your line of aim, take one pre-measured step forward, with that foot on the bridge arm side and carefully move into and form a comfortable stance behind the cue ball. Your feet should be approximately 45 degrees to the cue and the line of aim. Cue-tip should be close behind the cue ball and directly in the middle, the stroking forearm is hanging straight down from the elbow. Be concerned that your bridge hand to the cue ball is no greater than a handprint apart. Start soft and relaxed warm-up strokes, slowly and without overreacting. Begin a consistent, rhythmic and relaxed warm-up stroke while observing how straight you are moving the cue to the desired line of aim, another good reason for keeping the ferrule clean. At this point, you may observe where small adjustments are needed but normally you are becoming exceedingly comfortable with this sight picture. After two, three or four warm-up strokes to measure the speed of delivery and you have a comfortable sight picture up to this point, then stop the cue-tip close behind the cue ball. You are now separating the warm-up stroke from the follow-through stroke. Remember, this is the last examination you undergo before shooting. You must now question yourself whether the shot will turn out the way you imagined it would, or not. Be honest with yourself: "Am I aiming correctly and can I deliver this correctly?" These two questions have only one correct answer that should ever move you to deliver your follow-through stroke, "Yes". However, no considering should be made if the answer is not certain or otherwise negative, unless your intention is to see what it is you are doing wrong. Whether or not you can make it a "desired" outcome, should be kept relevant with success and ability. For the beginner this means, first get good at making the shot successfully and figure out where your problems lay through trial and error. Practice makes perfect, only if you practice perfectly. Therefore, follow these tips with perfect determination.

If however, everything is programmed for success, then pull the cue back smooth, evenly, consequently but relaxed, to the end of your programmed backstroke. Stabilize that elbow! At the crest of the backstroke, like a metronome (used to measure time in music) reaches its end to one side and begins back toward the other direction, slowly and deliberately, and gradually increasing speed, follow-through! At this point, you should be focused on only one thing. Although beginners and students of this game find this quite astonishing, what you are watching and concentrating on at this instant, is not the cue ball or the object ball anymore, but where and how far you throw the cue tip through the cue ball! After the cue tip comes to rest at the end of the follow-through, hold still and examine the tip position carefully. Remember, 8-12 cm through the cue ball and does the tip lead to the left or the right or is it perfectly in the middle, where it should be. At least for beginners, it is important to check and control the follow-through stroke always, but be honest and determined about this, more on this later.

3.2.1 How long should the pause be?

As we mentioned earlier, between the warm-up and follow-through stroke a player pauses to switch mentally his next intended move. How long should this pause be? Some are as long as three seconds and there are those who make no noticeable break in movement at all. Somewhere there in between, the rest of the players in the world are at home. Those professionals, who do not show any noticeable break in movement, have no problem with separating the warm-up from the follow-through stroke. Years of experience have led them to trust their own rhythm and instincts to the point where the warm-up and follow through appear to run fluidly together. Let that be their personal trait or style. The beginner on the other hand, observing this style is led to believe that this is something to immediately strive toward, but this is not entirely true. Many professionals show this separation before actual delivery.

The beginner should start with a distinct separation, up to 2 sec., then this gives them the time they need to register certainty before delivering the shot. It should be a prerequisite to call upon this certainty for every shot. In time, through repetition one begins to instinctively know how to approach and execute in a more relaxed manner, while still remaining fully concentrated. Being fully relaxed and fully concentrated is a trait any good pool player shows, when playing good. This complicated form of tapping your head and simultaneously rubbing your tummy is a bit more difficult for a beginner to master, because of the questions arising in the many new situations they encounter during play.

3.2.2 The warm-up stroke

The beginner should stay with three to four warm-up strokes during normal training shots. Later he should develop a definite rhythm and number the warm-up strokes at a constant level. A good "rule of thumb" would be, the greater the difficulty the greater number of warm-up strokes may be required. Every player will develop his or her rhythm sooner or later but be reminded, that it isn't the number of warm-up strokes that will help to make the shot but rather, how you address the situation in the beginning. Many players tend to handle the warm-up phase much to cautiously and then explode into the follow-through phase inexact and hasty, causing them to warp the original line of aim.

3.2.3 Missing

There isn't a person in the history, present or past, who doesn't miss a shot now and then. Be it a beginner or a full-blown professional. Naturally, the grave difference here is that the pro will miss many times more seldom than a beginner does. Our main interest during play, to put this simply is to (A) move the cue ball to the touching point or ghost ball and (B) achieve our objective with the object ball in a pocket and (C) land or "get shape" with our cue ball in the desired general area. If our objective is not achieved or only in part, then this is primarily due to an incomplete vision for the situation at hand.

3.2.4 A question of exactness

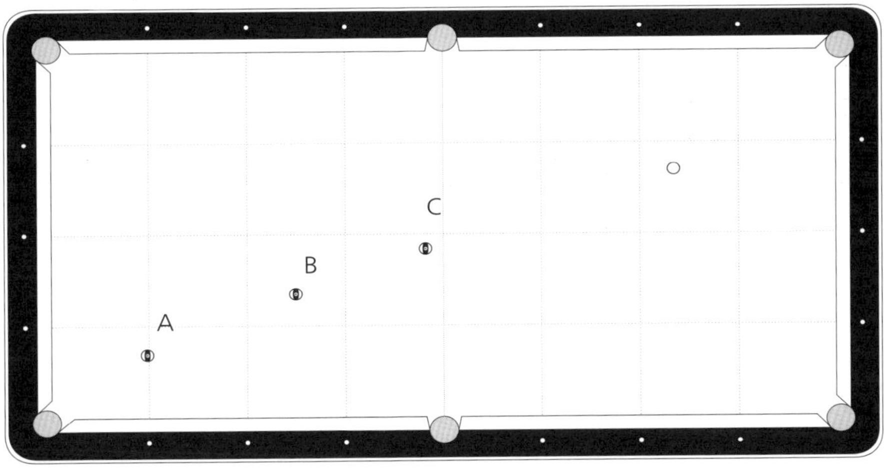

Diagram: 155

This brings us naturally to the point of exactness in pool billiards. Observe diagram 155 for a moment.

You see three different situations, which should relay to you three different grades of difficulty. Given the fact that the cue ball position remains constant, which of these three object ball situations would you rather have, if when achieved, you could win a brand new car? Regardless what happens with the cue ball afterwards, the object ball is at least pocketed in the corner pocket.

For the beginner it should be relatively clear, that situation A dominates your decision here. Then the closer the object ball is to the pocket, the bigger the margin of error becomes.

Taking a closer look at the margin of error, the two extreme touching points in diagram 156 are marked with "X". Anywhere between these two points are an innumerable number of possible touching points which would enable this ball to fall in this corner pocket. That means we have a margin of error covering better than 25 percent of the balls lateral diameter. Of course, the further the object ball is from the pocket, the smaller the margin of error becomes, the more exact your line of aim and refined your follow-through stroke must be.

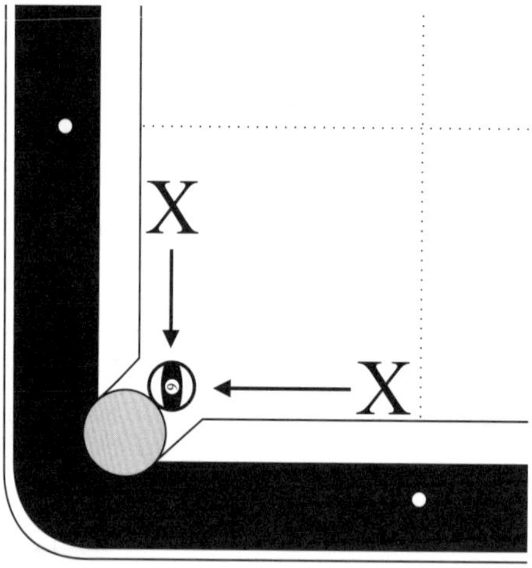

Diagram 156

However, this does not mean you should address those balls with a comfortable margin of error with any less assertiveness, rather look upon them as opportunities to focus upon better shape possibilities with much more clarity and extension.

We will explain a few options here.

One option would be: Striking this ball more or less fully, with draw action and steer the cue ball back short distances towards the middle of the table or parallel to the rail.

Another option is to strike the object ball thin with stop shot action. Depending on whether the cue hits the side or the end rail afterwards, a soft stroke (stroke speed 2), will send the cue ball normally to the other end of the table.

A third option would be to strike a good third of the possible striking range on the object ball with follow action (speed 2). The cue ball, after making the object ball and hitting the rail, will usually have enough follow action in it working against its course of movement away from the rail, to stop the cue ball dead in its tracks.

Try these three basic options and get to know them better. Soon you will realize which option has the best chance for generally all positioning distances on the table. You will also come to find out that there are more than just ***these three***. However, keep in mind that these three options are the easiest to control for a beginner with a good stroking technique and therefore options that should be at least mastered by anyone above this.

Another point which should be mentioned, that sometimes effects our exactness the higher it is raised is "stroke energy".

The higher the stroke energy the more difficult it is to achieve exactness.

3.2.5 Stroke energy

Stroke energy is defined at best, in the time it takes to drive the cue tip roughly 10 cm past, through that point where the cue ball was.

The shorter this time span is, the harder the cue ball has been hit.

There are a number of methods for measuring stroke energy. We will show two of them, starting with that which is most generally used. See diagram 157.

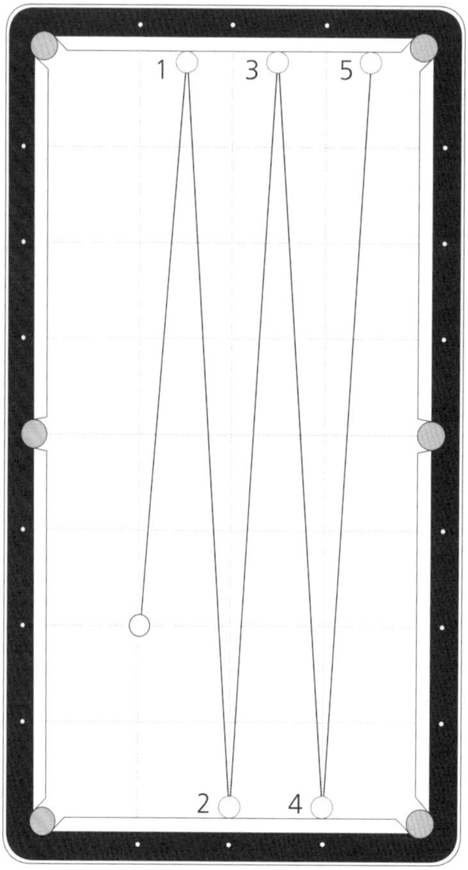

1 very light
2 light
3 medium
4 hard
5 very hard

Diagram 157

The second method can be described best when you view our graphic in diagram 158. This makes it easier to describe in words. On a scale from 1 to 10, where "10" is the absolute maximum stroke energy a player would be able to apply individually and would define his or her "break shot". The stroke energy "5" is 50 percent, half, medium or normal playing power.

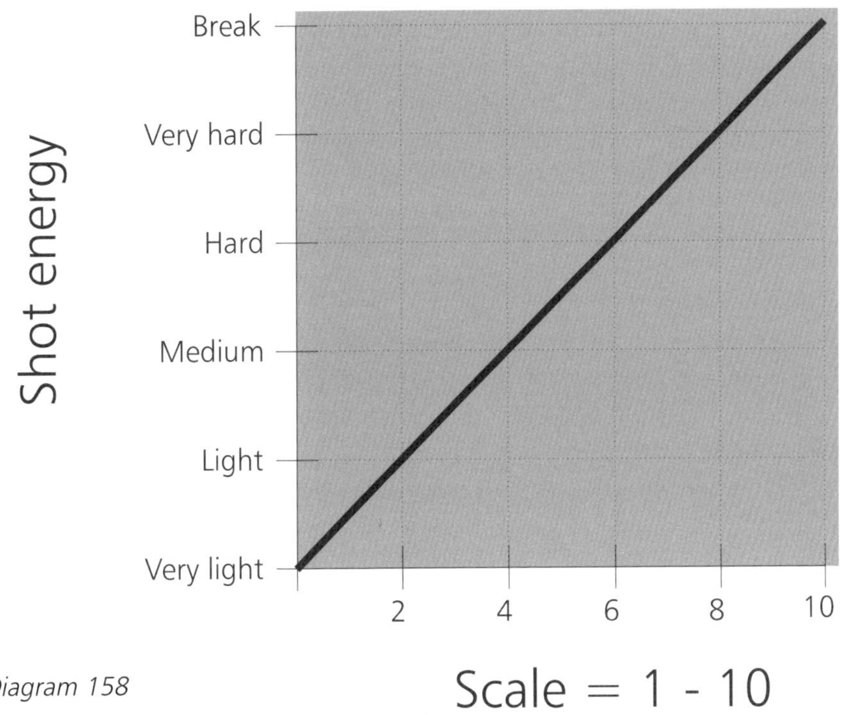

Diagram 158

However, because our scale is broken down in increments of 10%, it becomes increasingly unpractical the closer the "stroke energy" of "1" and under is come to. Then there will be situations where 10% of your stroke energy and less is required.

It is quite important that one understands and can visualize their stroke energy and define it practically beforehand. Knowing this allows you to imagine what will happen after the shot has been delivered and is a definite requirement for realizing and achieving shape for the next shot.

3.2.6 The ideal system

Look to our "aim and stroking" technique as a basic guideline to an ideal system in which over thirty years of observance and categorizing has been invested. Jerry Briesath has done this with the habits and traits of the best players in the world, to help give us a clear picture, which is important if you really intend to get better at this sport. Because of this, Jerry Briesath has become probably the most successful trainer, to date, in the world. Through his observance and categorizing, he has taken "this" or "that" excellent "trait" or "habit" and molded "hypothetically" the ***model*** or ***ideal player***, to which anyone can convert or strive toward in a shorter period than normal.

Systematic training concepts

To observe or play against any one professional, daily or at least often will certainly help the weaker players game extensively. However, in order to get even better than that particular talent you need diversified information, then you not only copy their good traits or habits but the bad ones as well. The Jerry Briesaths concept allows us to gain a window to the core of your problem. Something you can immediately see and correct or at least adapt to. The professional has learned to live with his own bad habits to the point where they're nothing more than jewelry to their own personal style and the beginner or weaker player who is given the chance to follow his lead and learn from the example presented will get to where the professional is eventually as well. However, the main problem here is the word "eventually". These, relatively few and unwise to follow examples, were earlier problem zones in their makeup that the professional now exhibits as their own personal style. The one swings his cue from the side, because when he was 6 years old, he didn't want to stand on a stool for every shot and just naturally kept using and refined this side arm technique, (F. Bustamente). The other just hated to waste time and can now run 15 balls off the table in less than a minute, (L. Butera). These are just a couple of extreme examples but if you attempt to copy them, it will take you as long or longer than it took them to get where they are now. Developing and integrating the guidelines we have presented here for an ideal aim and stroking system will allow you to develop your own style and help you to understand your basic problems and individual strengths faster so you can get to where the pros are sooner. Maybe just as fast or faster, good luck!

4. The stop shot

In many books and learning videos' on this subject, the student is often presented with the simple explanation, "To stop the cue ball, you must strike it in the middle. To draw the cue ball, strike it further underneath on its vertical axis and to have the cue ball follow, strike it above the middle on the vertical axis." For the hobby or casual player, this can be considered a good generalization that will help him for the first couple of months of play. Because the casual player is not normally interested in developing their game to the best possible level at the moment, they still come to realize during this period that there is a lot more to it than that!

The concrete description of a stop shot is nothing less than, "the entire „momentum transfer" from the cue ball to the object ball "in an instant". This will also mean, that once the cue ball has struck the object ball, it will remain exactly a ball diameter in front of where the object ball was laying. There are those, good meaning players who attempt to demonstrate this to a beginner "how to shoot a stop shot", but do not bring the cue ball to a complete standstill. This may cause the beginner to believe that the cue ball should take thereafter the earlier position or place that the

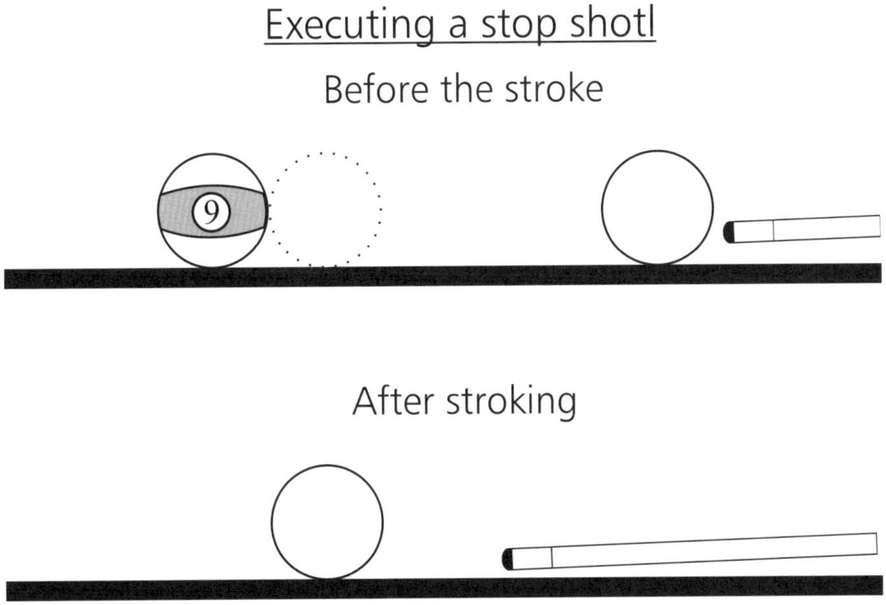

Diagram 159

object ball had been occupying. Wrong, then this is a placement ball, in which the cue ball had a chance to generate a small amount of follow before striking the object ball. Which in this case, may have been done more by accident than by design, but is no longer considered a stop shot in the perfect sense. However, the good meaning player is satisfied with this example.

4.1 Conditional ball consequence

In order to explain the unconditional momentum transfer (perfectly struck) of a correctly executed stop shot, the beginner needs to understand a little more about the mechanics of conditional consequence. A ball can be found or set in three basic types of conditions:

- The slipping condition
- The rolling condition and
- The still condition

4.1.1 The slipping condition

The slipping condition contains rotational or sliding characteristics' that will last longer the harder the ball is struck. The table surface or cloth has initially no immediate influence.

We define here in general, two types of slipping effects that can be applied to the cue ball:

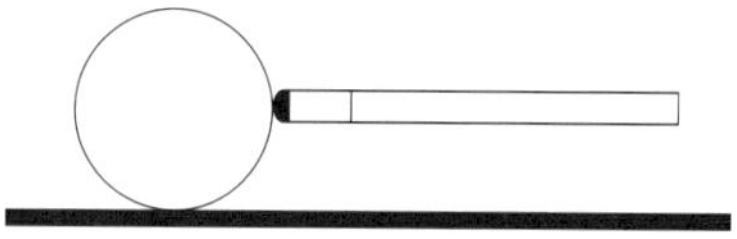

Diagram 160

- Striking the cue ball hard in the center
- Striking the cue ball hard above or below the center

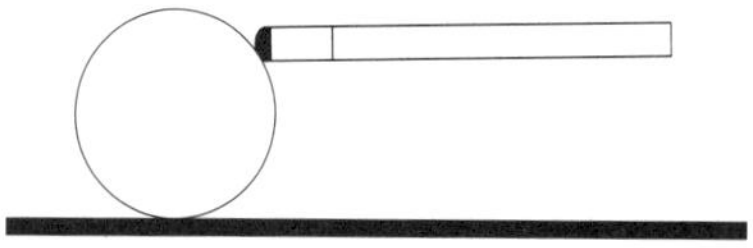

Diagram 161

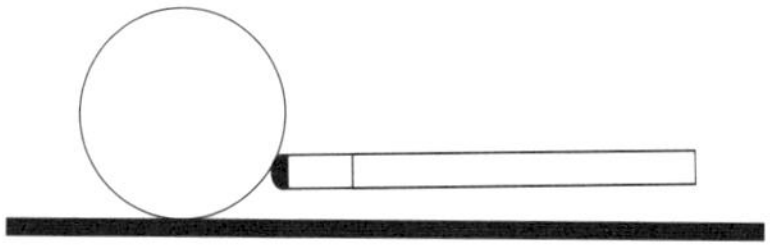

Diagram 162

In the first case, the cue ball, inside the distance of a meter will rotate eventually up to four times and less, depending on the condition of the cloth.

Diagram 163: If the cue ball is hit very hard in its center, it will complete fewer full rotations in a short distance. In the diagram, the dashed ball represents one full rotation.

In the second case, the cue ball, being struck either above or below the center can rotate on its vertical axis, forwards or backwards up to 20 times and more inside the same distance.

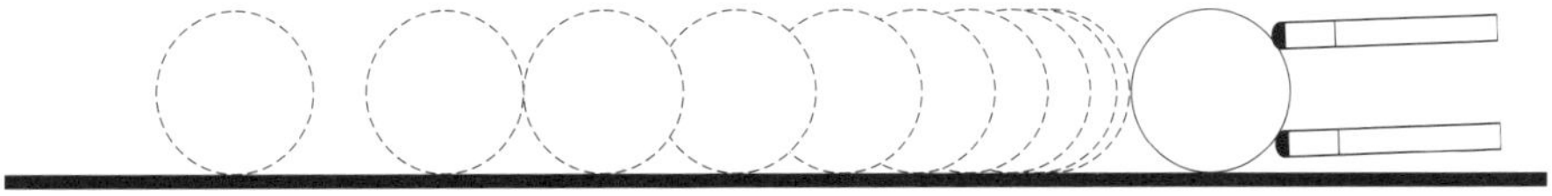

Diagram 164: If the cue ball is hit hard above or below the center, it will complete many full rotations in a short distance. In the diagram, each dashed ball represents a full rotation.

The point we wish to make here is that the cue balls actual diameter is not moving at a 1:1 ratio with the table surface initially. However, in time the table surface or cloth wants to bring all ball movement to a standstill eventually, regardless of how hard the ball was struck initially. Before this happens however, the ball will normally transfer itself into a rolling condition.

4.1.2 The rolling condition

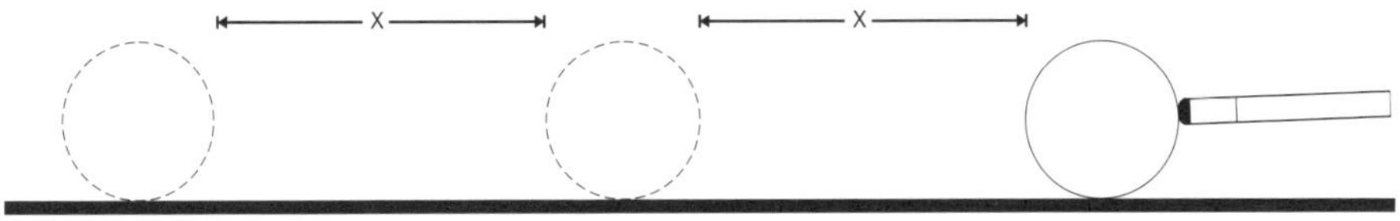

Diagram 165: Given enough distance, a ball set into motion will eventually or immediately move with a normal rolling momentum, regardless to where it was struck. The distance lines marked with „x" in the above diagram become constant. Each dashed ball represents a full rotation.

To the ball with a normal rolling momentum, it is said that the actual ball diameter is moving close to a 1:1 ratio with the table surface. Consequently, 5 cm of the balls partial circumference equals a distance of 5 cm that will cover the table surface. The actual diameter that a cue ball normally has is roughly 18 cm but will cover in one rotation, normally a bit more. In light of this much too often forgotten and/or misunderstood fact, it may now be easier for one to better imagine or vision, what went wrong and why.

4.1.3 The still condition

We understand of course, that every ball movement ends is a still condition. However, only in this condition is it possible to see points of contact with the naked eye. By using the numbering on the ball, the tone lines that separate different colors of the ball or the reflections on the ball, we can use this as helpful reference points for retaining the exact contact point on the object ball during the aim. More than this is not important other than this potential and definition.

4.2 Why the stop shot stops

The cue ball stops because it has no forward or draw energy after striking a given object ball and no deflection to the left or the right (the cue-ball strikes the object-ball squarely).

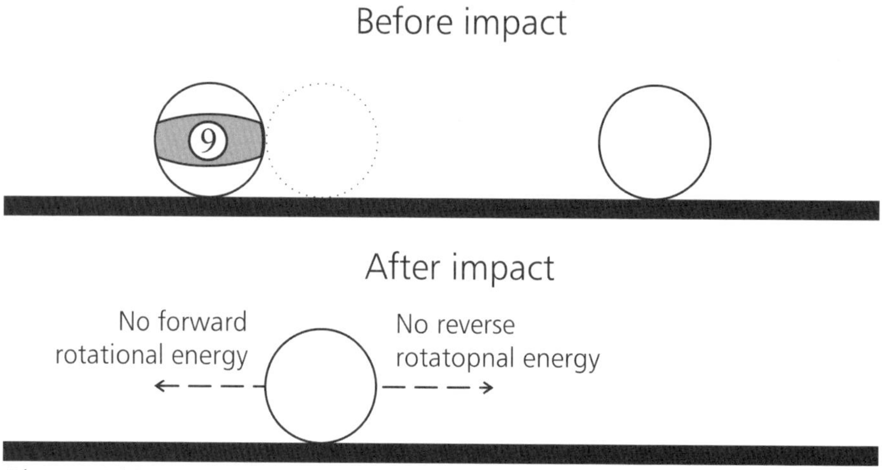

Diagram 166

We emphasize the fact however, that although all forward and draw energy is effectively neutralized and causes the cue ball to come to a stop, left or right English may cause the cue ball to turn horizontally on its own axis. We mentioned earlier the fact that any ball struck hard would initially begin with a sliding condition before stopping or eventually moving into a rolling condition where after it eventually comes to a resting or still condition that would conclude the shot.

Two powers are responsible for this:

- The balls own weight (gravitation)
- The cloth condition (resistance)

Because the resistance through „wind factor" against the ball aerodynamics plays such a small roll, we will ignore this completely.

How the stop shot functions has nothing to do with aerodynamics anyway. There are two facts that need to be realized and achieved before a stop shot can take place.

- The cloth surface will always work (old: relatively effective; new: relatively ineffective) against a sliding ball, to bring it into a rolling condition.
- During the distance between cue ball and object ball, the cue ball is not allowed to begin a rolling condition before hitting against the object ball. The cue ball must therefore be in a static sliding condition in that instant or it will not come to an immediate standstill.

In order to achieve correct action required for a standard stop shot over various distances, the cue tip must strike the cue ball on or below the horizontal axis in the middle or at various points on the vertical axis beneath together with various degrees of stroke energy. Diagram 167 shows the range on the cue ball that can be used for a stop shot. Because the vertical range of striking points on the cue ball is similar to those for a draw

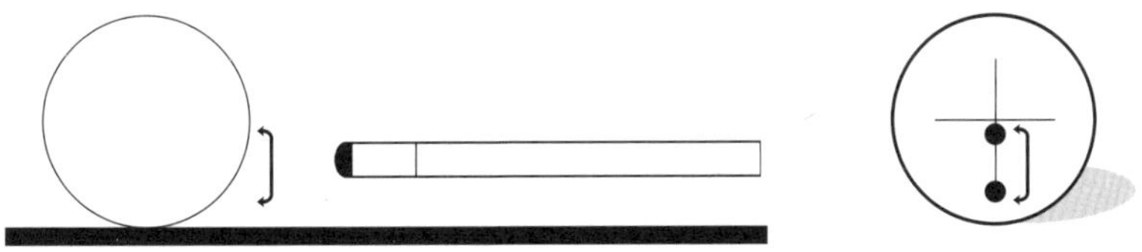

Diagram 167

shot, it becomes increasingly understandable why the want for one was replaced by the other. Mainly, because the required stroke energy was inadequate for that particular striking point on the cue ball. The range required for a stop shot encompasses the entire lower half of the cue ball, where the striking point moves lower and the stroke energy becomes higher the further away the object ball is to the cue ball. Therefore, two variables must be defined and understandably imagined in you, before the ideal stop shot can continuously be achieved.

- The stroke energy
- The striking point on the cue ball

These two variables are always dependent on one another. The following four examples describe the blending procedures for the same result.

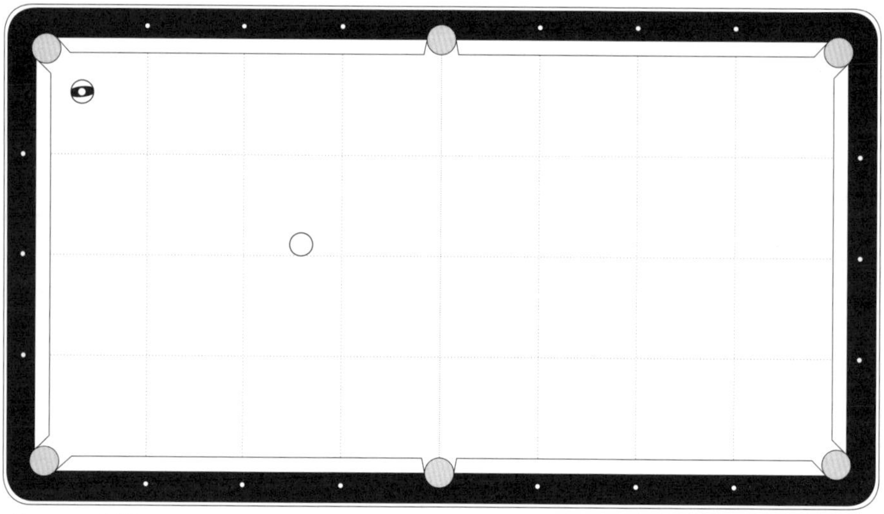

Diagram 168

Diagram 169: Stop shot with striking point shortly under the center of the cue ball – Shot velocity: 40 Km/h (24 mph) (40 Km/h is equivalent to around 80 to 90% of a 9-ball break). Here, the cue ball completes one complete rotation.

Diagram 169 shows the striking point being just under the cue ball center. In this case the stroke energy needs to be very high, roughly 40 km/h (24 mph). The cue ball will achieve one complete retroactive rotation before beginning to slide and stop upon contact with the object ball.

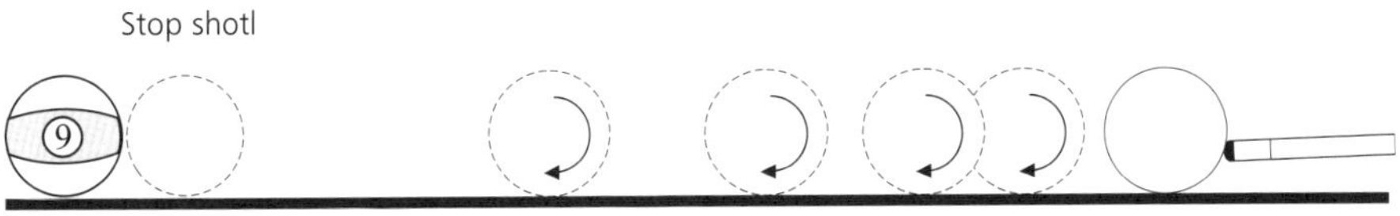

Diagram 170: Stop shot with a low striking point on the cue ball – Shot velocity: 30 Km/h (18 mph). In the diagram, each dashed ball represents a full rotation.

Diagram 170 uses a striking point just under our last example. In this case, our stroke energy needs to be some what less, roughly 30 km/h (18 mph). Here the cue ball will rotate roughly four times before beginning its slide and again stop upon contact with the object-ball.

The stop shot

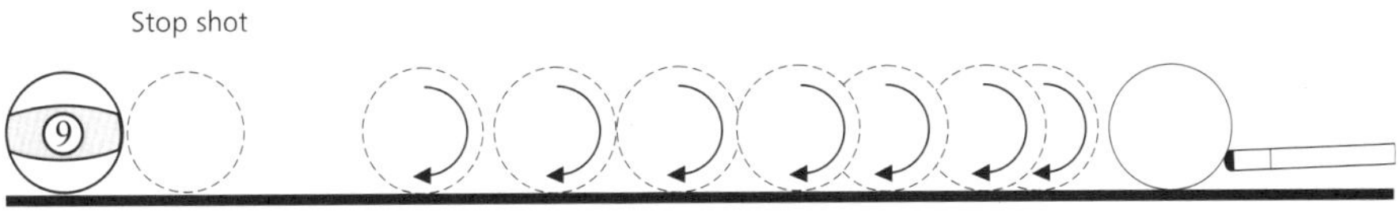

Diagram 171: Stop shot with a lower striking point on the cue ball – Shot velocity: 20 Km/h (12 mph). In the diagram, each dashed ball represents a full rotation.

For this example, the striking point is even lower and the stroke energy should be around 20 km/h (12 mph). Here the cue ball will achieve a retroactive rotation between six and eight times before sliding shortly and stop against the object ball.

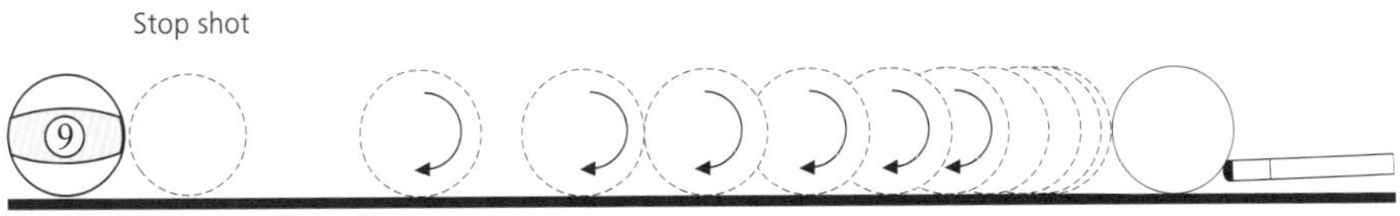

Diagram 172: Stop shot with the lowest striking point on the cue ball – Shot velocity: 10 Km/h (6 mph). In the diagram, each ball represents a full rotation.

In our last example, diagram 172, the striking point is at its lowest and just short of the 1 cm slip-zone. Here our stroke energy is around 10 km/h (6 mph) whereby the cue ball before beginning to slide and stop against the object-ball, will complete full reverse spins of some 15 times. Many refer to this sort of shot as a "soft stop".

In the following illustration, we use the numbers from our scale (diagram 158) in parenthesis () to describe required stroke energy.

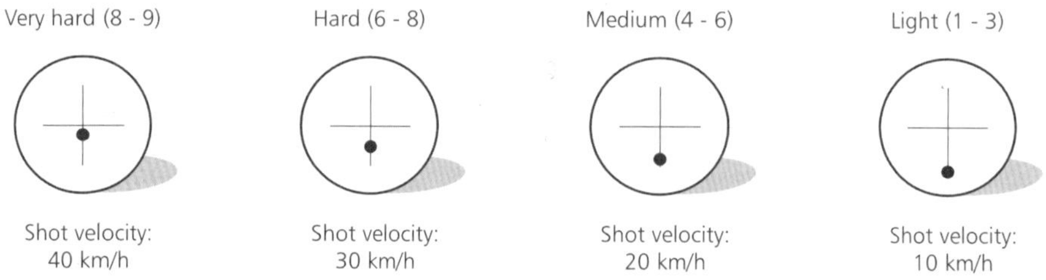

Diagram 173

The stop shot

If you recall, on our scale from 1 to 10 referring to stroke energy, 10 is the hardest (Break-shot) and 5 is a medium stroke or half the energy required for breaking.

The situations we outlined earlier for making a stop shot can more expressed simply in the following statement:

The lower the striking point on the cue ball is the lesser stroke energy will be required.

This statement serves the purpose of describing the dependent factors of "stroke energy" to "striking point" (for a stop shot, in the center or lower) for identical situations. Further, it should be mentioned that although our example refers to only four striking points, the professional on the other hand, may register up to 20 striking points for the same stop shot.

4.2.1 The mechanics of the stop shot

To better understand and visually witness the mechanics of the stop shot, it would be best to acquire an "old" striped object ball and practice the following situation described in diagram 174.

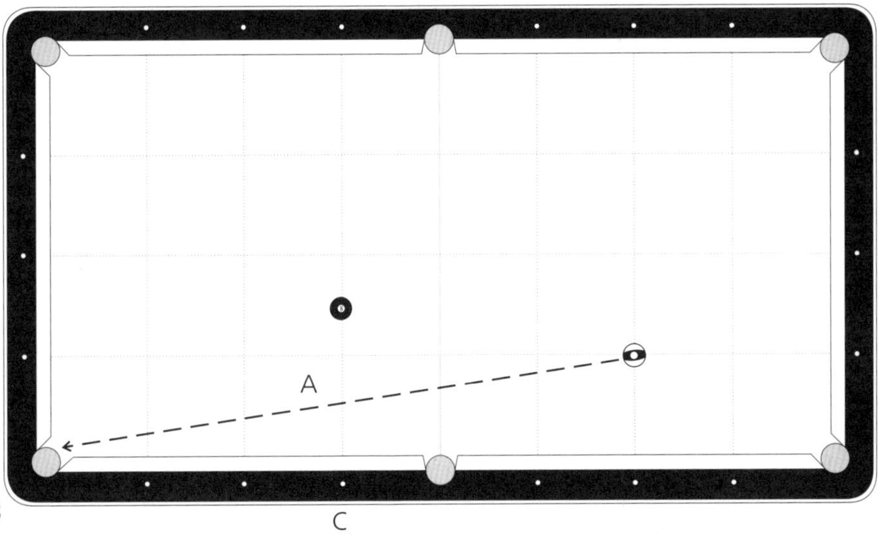

Diagram 174

Place the striped object ball before you as in diagram 175 with the stripe horizontal to the direction aimed.

This ball will represent the cue ball and should be aimed at the corner pocket (B). Place the black 8-ball parallel to line A at the height of the second diamond. Your mission, should you decide to accept it: At the point a little before and a little past parallel to where the 8-ball is and along line A, make the "striped" cue-ball skid and represent a stop shot.

Diagram:

For this exercise, aim low and use little stroke energy. Be careful of course of the 1 cm slip zone ring around the "striped" cue ball and observe what happens.

What should happen is described as follows:

The stop shot

At first, the stripes will swirl unrecognizably in reverse as it moves away. The closer the ball comes to the distance of where the 8-ball is laying, (parallel to you line of aim) the more the stripes on the ball become recognizable.

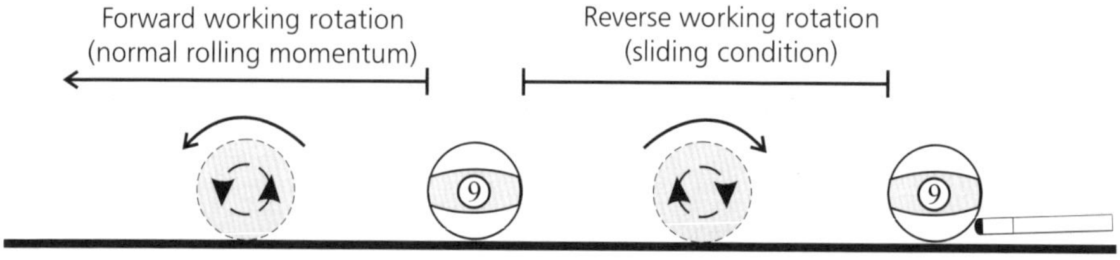

Diagram 176: During the transition from reverse working into a forward working rotation of a striped ball, one can identify the flipping effect to its stripe and just make out the number (here the yellow and white 9-ball) on the ball. If a ball where directly in the path at the point this transition came about, the ball would come to a sudden standstill.

The stop shot

Shortly before the striped ball goes by the 8-ball it should loose all of its reverse rotational energy or draw action and begin to slide or skid so that, for a fraction of a second, the ball number can be read on it. This slide or skid should carry on a little before and a little past the place where the striking point on the 8-ball would have been, were it on line "A" as well (see diagram 177).

This happens quite quickly for the human eye. It may be registered only as a change in rotational direction. If you were to film this exercise and watch the replay in slow motion, the point where the "slide" started and ended, would be clearly visible and can of course be better graded. During this "slide", the cue ball, outside of its own forward movement, has no other form of influencing energy. A "spherically still weight" of the same greatness and density, placed exactly in the path of our sliding weight or "spherically still, sliding weight" will receive from it the only thing it has left to offer; "movement". Thereafter, the cue ball will be left with nothing but its own "still weight" regardless of the velocity it was traveling at up to that instant and stops completely at that point, where the similar obstacle was initially reached or as in our case, exactly a ball diameter behind where the object ball was laying.

The point of this exercise is: repetition! Doing something over and over again will always give you more answers than you usually had questions for and certainly more answers than any author could list in a book

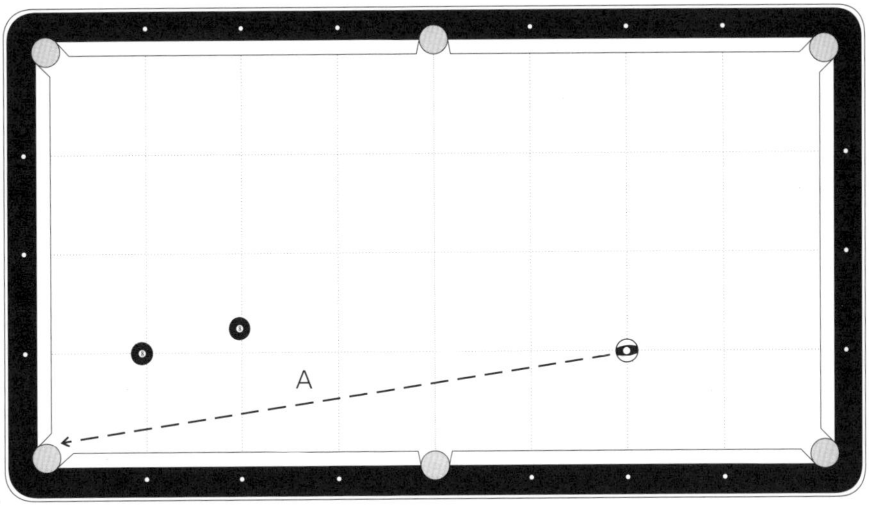

B

Diagram 177

on this sport, when considering the mental capacity this sport has to offer. However, by taking a look at your inconsistencies, when shooting a ball past the 8-ball like this, you don't need to setup anymore balls than the one you're shooting in the corner pocket, just grab the next one. And, you concentrate not only on the direction you are shooting, but also the distance the stop shot is taking place at. This exercise is variable.

4.2.2 The stop shot using constant stroke energy

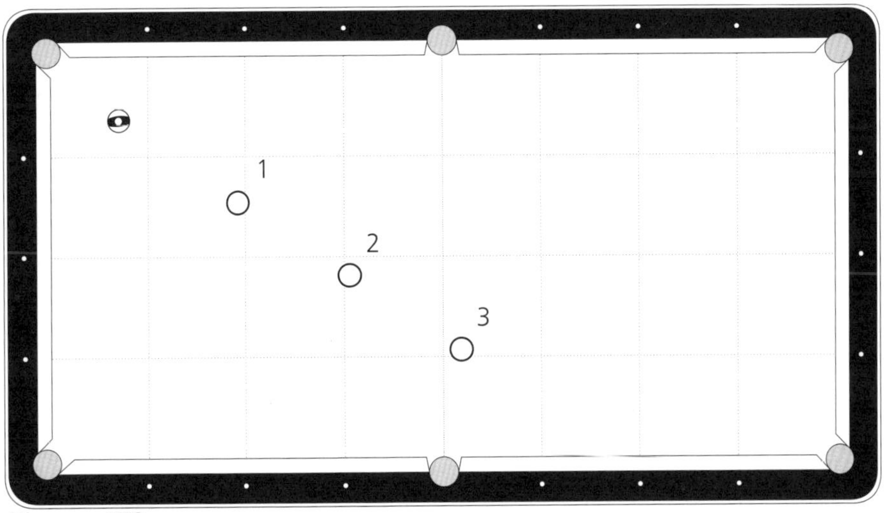

Diagram 178

In diagram 178, we want to achieve stop or slide action for three different distances. This exercise involves stroke energy on our scale between 3 and 4 or 30% to 40% of our maximum stroke energy, stay inside of this range.

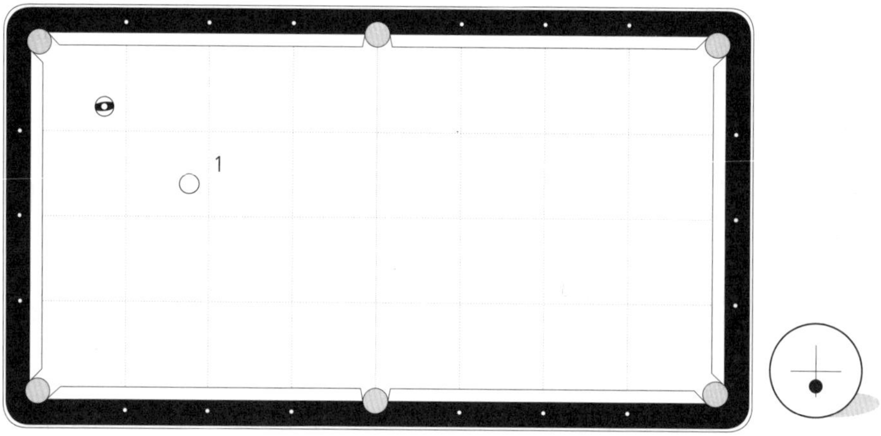

Diagram 179

Taking the first example, choose a striking point on the cue ball where you believe the „stop action" will take effect perfectly. This striking point will be somewhere between, shortly below its center and its lowest possible striking point on the cue ball. Because experience has shown us, that due to ball and cloth conditions and your idea of stroke energy vary to some degree, we will refrain from being explicit but go on to say, that the striking point lays somewhere between these two extremes. Putting this into practice, find this point and lock it firmly in your memory. Execute the shot with the same stroke energy you intend to use for the next two exercises later.

Before one can master this shot, you will experience four different cue ball reactions. To reinforce any suspicions you may have and/or questions we will explain each possible reaction that happen on occasion.

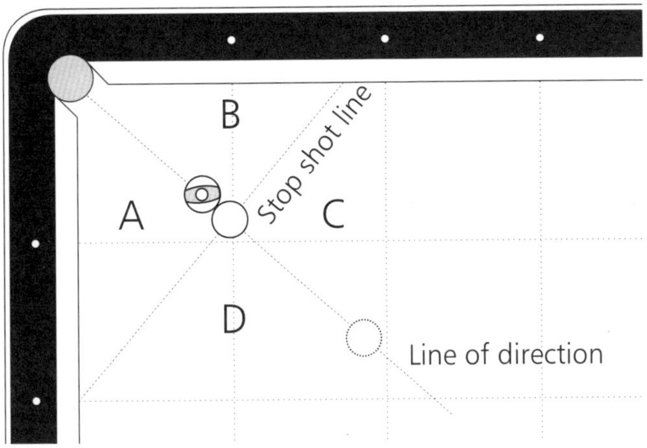

Diagram 180

Reaction 1: The cue ball stopped exactly a ball diameter behind where the object ball was laying. You found, at the onset, the correct striking point on the cue ball and executed the shot with the correct stroke energy required for your training environment. If your stroking technique is very good and you can remember the correct striking point and required stroke energy, you should be able to achieve identical cue-ball reactions continuously.

The stop shot

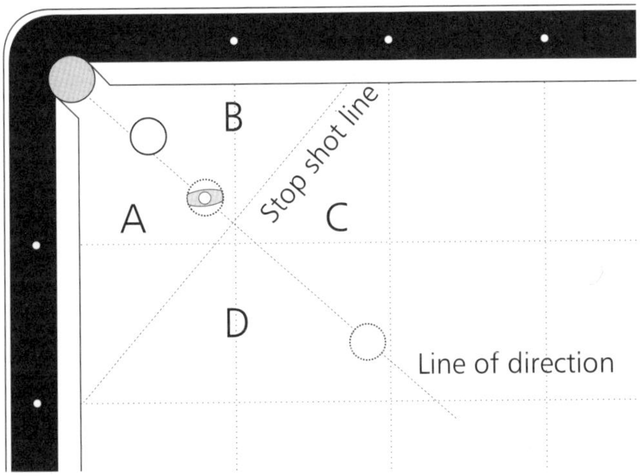

Diagram 181

Reaction 2: The cue ball follows the object ball and lands somewhere between the area of A and B on the line of aim. You had chosen a striking point on the cue ball that was higher than in reaction one. If after the shot, the cue ball also rolls off the line of aim, then a couple of additional possibilities are responsible for this.

a) The object-ball was not struck exactly in the middle and/or
b) The cue ball was struck with additional English.

Reaction 3: The cue-ball draws back from the object ball and lands somewhere between the area of C and D on the line of aim. Here you have

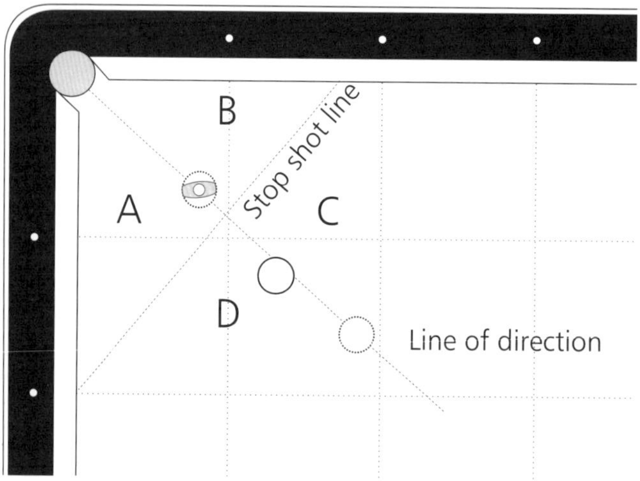

Diagram 182

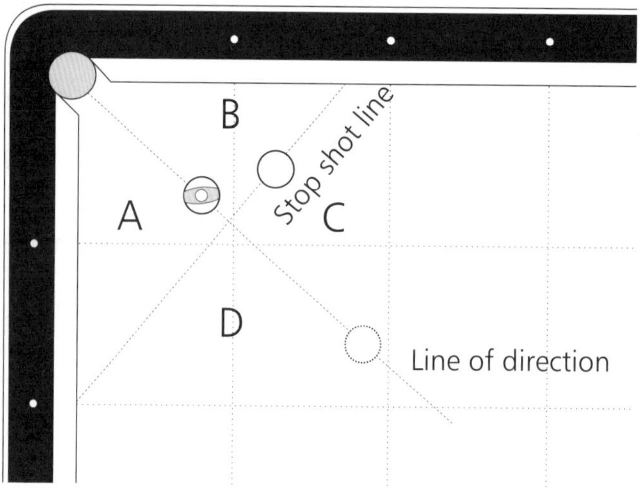

Diagram 183

The stop shot

chosen a striking point on the cue ball that was lower than in reaction one. If the cue ball veers off the line of aim here as well, then the „additional possibilities" of reaction two are the reason for this.

Reaction 4:

The cue ball stays exactly a ball diameter behind where the object ball was but is spinning on its vertical axis. If after the shot, the cue ball moves 90°, to either the left or the right as well, then as funny as it may sound, this is also considered a stop shot. However, this is moreover a tool for cheating the pocket. If you observed closely, then you also witnessed that in the direction the cue-ball was spinning or on that side to which the cue-ball was struck with English, the object-ball had traveled in the opposite direction or pocket side. This can backfire to the point where the object ball is thrown completely off the desired path to the pocket. Whereby, the cue ball stops but the English it was given, grabbed the object ball and simply threw it off-line and you miss the shot. On the other hand, this can be very useful when a particular shot is not quite on line with the intended pocket and cue-ball shape in this area is useful. We speak here of "holding the cue-ball".

Leaning on your reproducible playing system, practice each of these distance examples five times, out of which at least three of each are successful. Remember to use the same stroke energy for all. Notice where the striking point on the cue ball is for each of these three distances. The further apart the cue ball is from the object ball, the lower this striking point on the cue ball, of course will be.

4.2.3 The stop shot using a constant striking point on the cue-ball

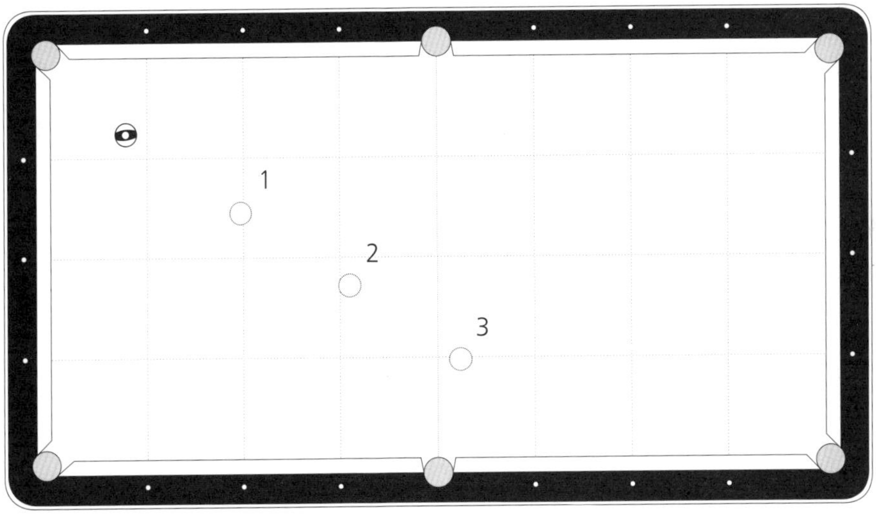

Diagram 184

The stop shot

In diagram 184, we intend to describe further how the same results can be achieved using a different technique, in this case variable velocity. Decide here on using the lowest striking point on the cue ball that you used for the third distance of the previous exercise. For the other two distances in this exercise, you need only to vary your stroke energy. Therefore, the closer you are to the object ball the lesser stroke energy is required.

Given the fact that you use a reproducible playing system, the beginner, believing he is doing everything right, finds here an enlightening problem with the first of these three distance exercises. The problem here being; that „roughly 8-12 cm past that point where the cue ball was laying, with the cue tip" problem. A seemingly correct follow-through stroke,

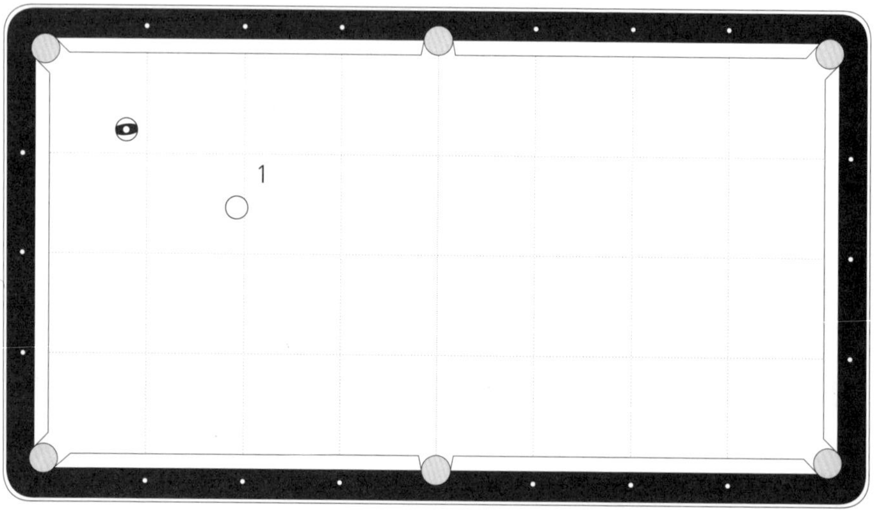

Diagram 185

The stop shot

refuses to produce the stop shot character that is wanted, but brings about unwanted draw action. Many players respond to this by breaking off their follow-through or cut off abruptly the distance they normally travel through the cue ball. Here, they give prize to their faulty technique. Being able to cheat the pocket is a good weapon, but to cheat your playing system is not wise. The player should always recognize the situation he is reading and conform his playing system to it. If you recall in chapter three on "Technique", 3.1.1.5 "roughly 10 cm past" then we must also show the parallel in technique deviation between the billiard and golf player (diagram 186). When the golfer "tees off" for a distance of 200 meters, his back swing is equivalent to his follow-through, whereby the club head will start and end over each shoulder for the follow-through stroke. However, if the golfer needs only to move the ball over a short distance to the cup, he won't rear back as he would for teeing off and stop abruptly for the putt but rather use only that amount of back swing for the distance required. If the golfer were to do this, the body control he would need to use to brake

Diagram 186

the follow-through for the last 20 cm to the golf ball would not allow him to coordinate the correct line of aim. Your follow-through distance should simply equal the back swing.

In our second exercise here however, using a soft stroke, you should be able to follow-through normally again, 8-12 cm or roughly 10 cm past, at the same low striking point.

Complete this exercise as you did in the preceding sector, observing as you did previously where the cue ball comes to rest and get good at this.

These two exercises for the stop shot have also been integrated in the chapter on "training". By this however, we intend to show the learning student, how the individual dependence between stroke energy to striking point on the cue ball for the same situation is, as well as the related dependence, the "distance" between the object and cue ball will have.

Keep this in mind:

For one and the same "stop shot", the striking point on the cue-ball must be lowered when the stroke energy is lowered and vice versa.

For increasing distances between cue and object ball, either the stroke energy is raised or the striking point is lowered on the cue ball to achieve a stop shot effect.

4.3 The draw shot

The draw shot hits the object ball with more spin energy as the stop shot.

The draw shot contains the basic principle of the stop shot hit initial stage. We wish to support this definition with the following statement.

In diagram 184 of the preceding sector, we have our stop shot exercises, look to exercise number 3. Here we needed to strike very low on the

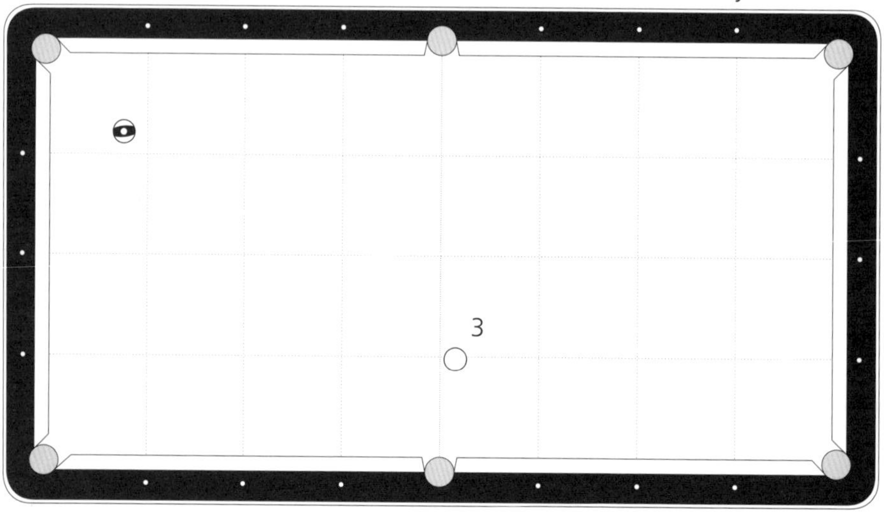

Diagram 187

cue ball. If we apply the **exact same "Technique"** that was required for a stop shot in that exercise, for this exercise in diagram 188, you will find that the cue ball will draw back toward you.

The distance between cue and object ball has been shortened enough that the first stage a stop shot normally has, is kept active after hitting the object ball. Through the contained abundance of reverse slippage and the

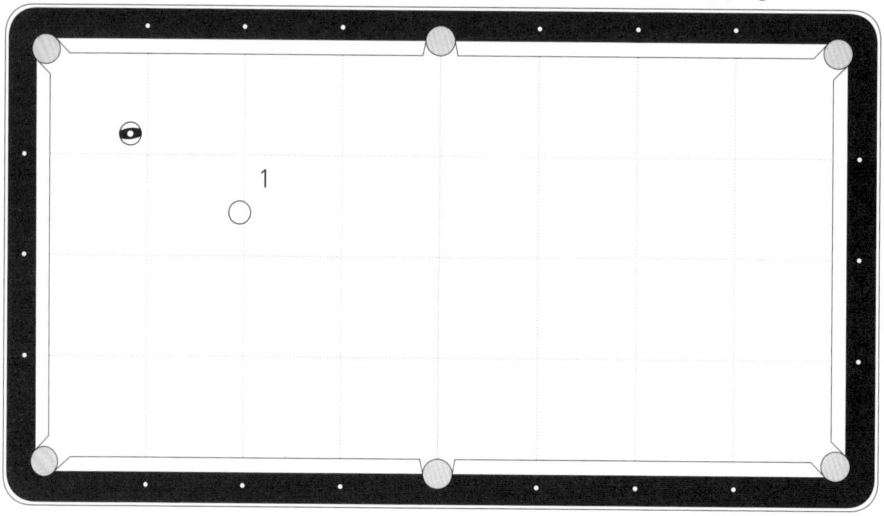

Diagram 188

shortened range between both balls. By using the same Technique and power we used for a stop shot, we get a "real" draw action on the cue ball. Similar distances are covered in both cases. Realizing this can be very useful and a good reason why the stop shot should be mastered and tailored to your playing system first. However, as one can well see, the draw shot is not in a class of its own but simply a modified stop shot with a heck of a lot of reverse slippage. The important measure for obtaining a draw shot with abundant reverse slippage are:

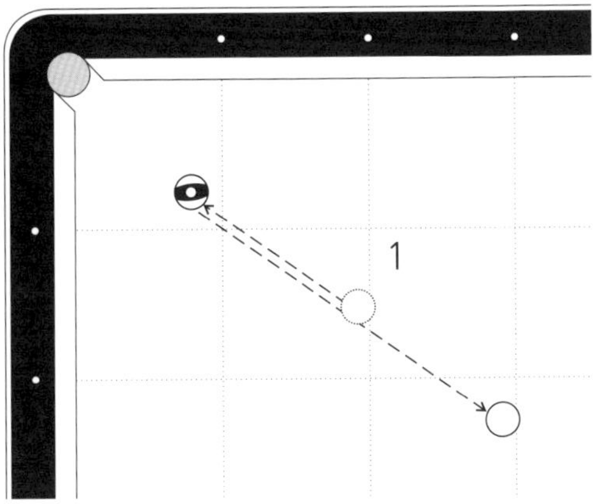

Diagram 189

1. The cue tip travels well past where the cue ball was.
2. The further the striking point on the cue ball is lowered from its center, the higher amount of draw energy can be achieved.

Many students come to our course with the following declaration: "I don't have a problem with the stop shot, only with drawing the cue-ball." Afterwards, it becomes increasingly clear to them that they were viewing this matter from the wrong standpoint. Those who have problems with the draw shot have not completely mastered or even understood the basic principles and/or striking energy necessary for executing a stop shot in order to modify it effectively.

To conclude, the following rule for executing a draw shot apply:

For one and the same striking point on the cue ball: The higher the stroke energy is the further back the cue ball will travel.

For one and the same stroke energy to the cue-ball: The lower the striking point on the cue-ball is, the further back the cue ball will travel.

The further away the cue ball is from the object ball, the more the above two maxims need to be maximized so that the original position for the cue ball or more can be reached.

4.4 The follow shot

We describe two types of follow shots, which are chiefly separated through the type of technique applied to the cue ball.

1. The cue-ball is struck at a striking point over and above its center, or

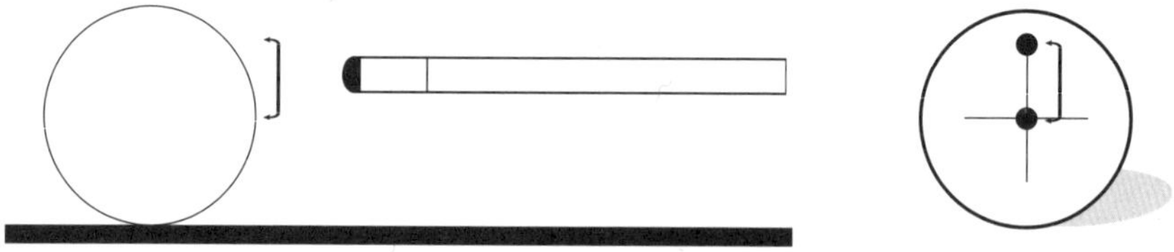

Diagram 190

2. The cue ball is struck at a striking point on or under its center.

In our first case, where the cue ball is struck above its center, (given a level cue delivery) no stop or draw action can be achieved. By striking the cue ball in this area, the cue ball can be influenced to roll forward as close to natural as possible. The higher the stroke energy is the greater the cue-ball slips or slides during this distance. Whereby, the cue ball spinning ratio to the table surface is faster initially, than it is movement.

The diagram below, attempts to demonstrate three different speeds and the typical reaction of the cue ball for each of them. The stuttered half-ball lines intend to depict the cue ball in its initial stage of forward slippage.

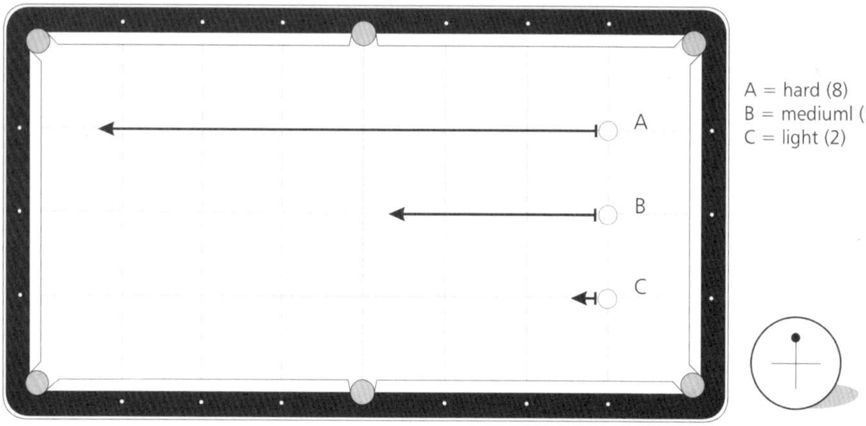

Diagram 191: Time length for the slide phase of the cue ball with different stroke speeds.

In this type of follow shot, using high stroke energy, the cue ball moves from its initial forward slippage condition eventually into a normal forward rolling condition.

Hitting the cue ball in this area with excessive force will invariably cause the cue ball to spring slightly. Whereas the distance covered can be said to be more "airborne", than not. The reason for this is simple and though this takes place faster than the eye or maybe another sense in you can register, it should be known. When executing this type of follow shot with excessive force, one strikes the cue ball at all times above its horizontal axis. Even with a level cue delivery, the cue-tip strikes the cue ball initially from above however slight. Through excessive force from above, plus a hard slate table surface below, the cue ball has to take the path of lesser resistance, in this case "up". This phenomenon and other hidden considerations will be covered more extensively in our next book.

Let us deal now with our second type of follow shot. Whereby, once the beginner finds he can utilize this shot under pressure, effectively, should no longer be considered a "beginner" in the perfect sense. Normally, all beginners and most casual or hobby players are unaware of this type of technique. Nevertheless, this technique is included among the fondest weapons in a professional's arsenal. The major reason for its usage is to

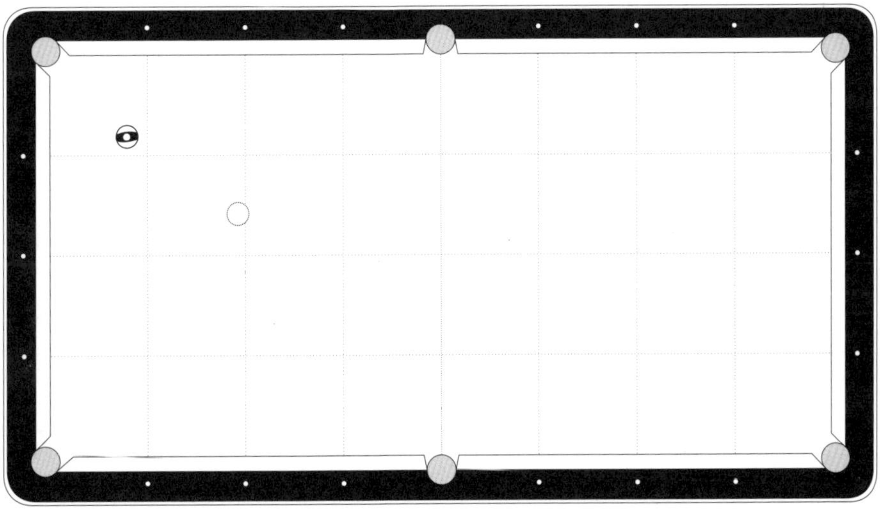

Diagram 192

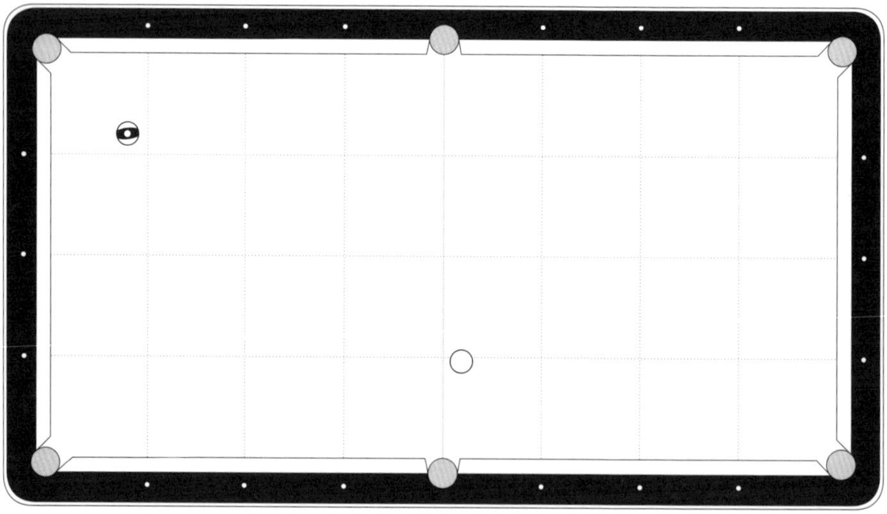

Diagram 193

The stop shot

take speed out of the cue ball over a greater distance before it touches the object ball and cut down the natural, further, forward movement in the cue ball to a minimum after the object ball has been struck.

In this case, our follow shot is a "stop-shot" with abundant forward rotation.

Notice:

The stop shot

Notice:

5. Training

When standing at the table, the player will find himself in one of three situations:

- When he trains alone
- When he trains with an opponent and
- When he participates in a tournament

One trains to better their technique, tactics, or special shot capabilities. This is usually accomplished alone or better with a trainer that can point out specific faults and help them to eliminate this effectively.

When playing with an opponent, outside of a tournament atmosphere, one attempts to prove ones own ability against their peers by showing their learned abilities and putting them to test. These mistakes are not graded too harsh, when it's a friendly game and they should eventually be stored for future reference toward hopeful elimination.

Under actual tournament conditions, one becomes officially graded by their peers. Here one strives to play their best game and learn to remember everything they were taught or have learned up to this point and put it to use effectively.

5.1 Sensible training

Practice alone doesn't make perfect. Perfect and sensible training makes perfect.

Some time ago, we met with a self-named trainer with reputedly much experience. The kids between the ages of 12 and 16 years were busy tackling the following situation: make the 8-ball and get shape on the 9-ball:

The reason such training is not sensible:

Experienced pool players are familiar with the difficulties this situation presents, even as a practice shot. However, the real reason is not the grade of difficulty (which one can find in Billiard Magazines and books on this

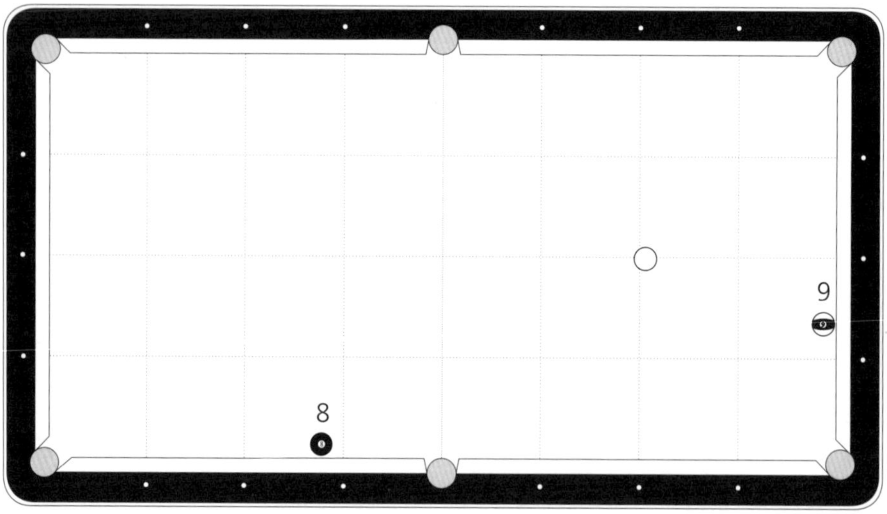

Diagram 194

subject) that catapults this issue under terms of illogical training, it's the *order of priority*.

Training

Certainly, the beginner is interested in getting to "the meat of the matter", when it comes to practicing on their game, and they won't be satisfied until they complete the shot, no matter how long it takes. Sooner or later, the situation is completed, probably with heavily applied body English and questionable shape. Once accomplished thereafter, they may be able to satisfy this job regularly 2 out of 10 times, maybe even three during training. However, such a meager average in training will be nonexistent under normal tournament conditions. The goal toward sensible training is to be able to satisfy successfully a given situation 9 out of 10 times. To reach this goal, one cannot put results ahead of everything else in the beginning. Power oriented training is more effective than result oriented in the long run. Then power oriented training means that you come before the balls (i.e. situation). Result oriented means the balls come before you and maybe even before you are ready. Beginners, as a rule are usually not result oriented. Beginners, who want to develop their game quicker, must first develop their coordination between the "cue stick" – "the hand" – "and the eye" (in short: the mechanics of their technique must be mastered). Before you can understand a situation, you must learn how to successfully "act" against it.

It is therefore imperative for the beginner to develop and utilize a good, solid playing system (mastering the mechanics of your technique).

Many players think that training and playing pool is the same, therefore, it's enough to play a couple-three hours a day with a friend. That may be, if you have reached a certain level of play or are one of the very few who do not need a high training program. However, this is not the rule. The distribution: Training – Playing – Tournament, for every level of play and every player, will vary greatly.

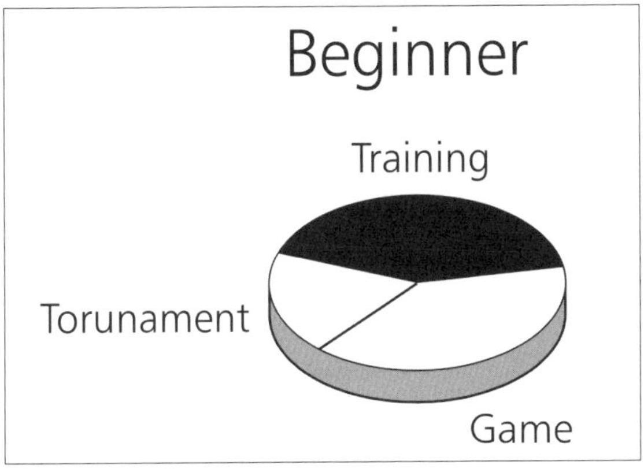

Diagram 195

The beginner should start by developing his basic "aim and stroking" technique and consequently put this to use during play. Only 20% of the time a beginner spends during play, should involve tournament participation. The reason for this is mainly, to experience better players in action and to sniff a little of that tournament atmosphere.

Training

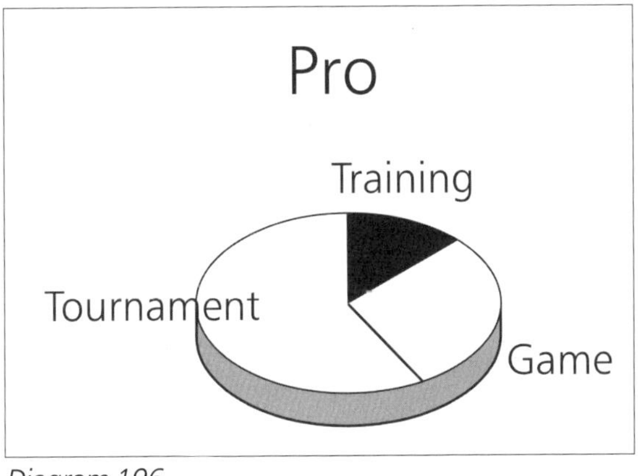

Diagram 196

As for professionals, the amount of time they will spend on "actual training" is quite a bit less, than of course, a beginner needs to spend. To get right down to it, his training has more to do with warming up basic movements and fine-tuning an already good technique. Most of his time is spent at tournaments and general play.

Diagram 197

By direct comparison to a typical league player, much more time is concentrated on Match play and less time on training and participates regularly at tournaments and championships.

Diagram 198

The hobby or free-time player, for that matter is really only interested in playing the game itself. He may participate in a small, hometown tournament, but will normally stay inside friendly levels of play with buddies of similar strength.

Naturally, there are a great number of players who cannot be categorized along the lines of the previous player description. Everyone is free to regulate their own training Pentium, because proven progress will depend greatly on the amount and frequency of highly competitive play and tournament participation. However, in the beginning, the more often the player participates in tournaments, the greater the sum in normal play and training there should be. Weaker players, along these guidelines, should work more on training than playing.

5.2 Practising

A basic training program and the practicing that is relative to this, should of course, serve the purpose of developing general technique. Practical exercises can be found in a variety of books on this subject, magazines or can be self-created. We have also taken it upon ourselves, to offer a string of practical exercises. They begin quite easy and graduate in difficulty. Passing from one level to the next, should be done first, when the previous level is completely mastered. Don't be too proud to drop back a level when the exercise you have graduated to becomes too difficult. Because practical exercises are most effective through inclination (easy to hard), small steps to these exercises require a high concern in movement technique. Naturally, big steps require a much greater concern. For a novice, the first attempt is usually too difficult to achieve. Through the following exercises, when a ball is pocketed, the cue ball is made to stop, follow or draw. The primary objective should always be kept in the forefront: Refinement of a reproducible basic playing system.

In order to achieve progress in this area, one should not make the mistake of relating the goals here with those that come forth in actual tournament play. Training, especially for the stroke, should have no tactical content in the beginning. Students need to concentrate fully on an aggressive offense. In this manner, one is better able to develop and study what is required for purifying their technique. Should things not turn out as you expected them to, then you need to study the ball movement much more closely and realize what they are trying to show you.

Training

A student of Jerry Briesath complained to him once during training, after confusingly shaking his head by saying: "Jerry, you told me; if I want to make a long draw, then I need to strike the cue-ball at its lowest point. I aimed low on the cue-ball, but I only came up with a stop shot!" Jerry reminded him by saying: "Whitey never lies...."

5.2.1 Exercises

Essentially, we have presented the most important exercises here. Naturally, they can be varied endlessly, so be careful not to get "one-sided" during these exercises. By this, we mean: when practicing a given example on the left side of the table, the same exercise should be inverted for the right side of the table as well.

Exercise 1: Shoot the object ball, from the head spot, directly into the adjacent corner foot pocket.

The goal of this exercise:

- Separate the process between the warm up stroke and the follow-through stroke
- Stroke straightness
- Elbow stabilization
- Remembering to stroke to and through the ball regular-ly

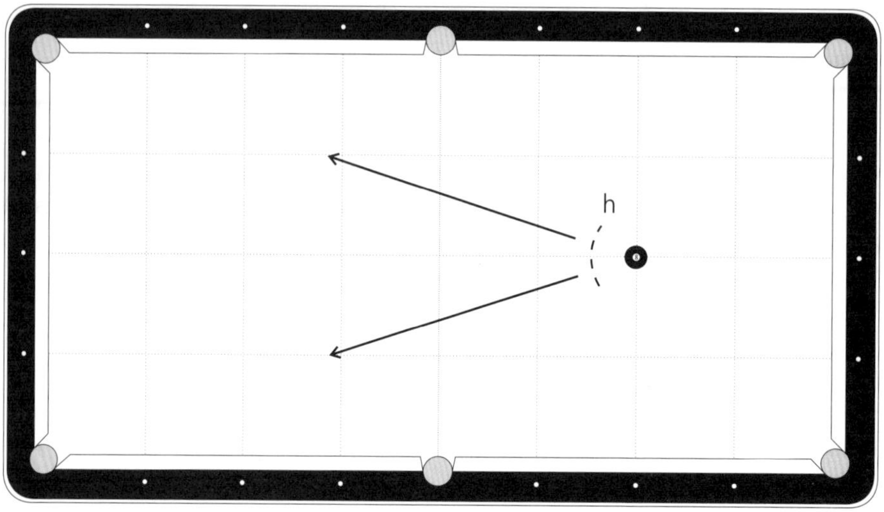

Diagram 199

Place the ball on the head spot and roughly 10 cm past it, mark a half ring (h) with chalk. This "half ring" is of course used to help control the distance the cue tip should pass through the cue ball. Play this ball in the left as well as the right pocket.

Vary the speed, using our stroke energy scale, between "2" and "4" (light to medium).

Concentrate on keeping the warm-up and follow-through stroke separated, with a self-designed pause. After executing the shot, freeze and answer these questions:

- Is the cue-stick covering the head spot? (straightness)
- Does the tip dive, when striking the cue ball with follow, stop, or draw to the table surface? (Elbow stabilization)
- Is the distance the cue-tip passes through the cue ball, constantly the same? (Elbow stabilization & stroking through the ball)

Exercise intensification:

- Increase your stroke energy up to stroke energy "7" (hard)
- Strike the cue ball on its vertical axis – apply "follow", "stop" and "draw" action
- Vary the angle the cue ball is aimed from
- Shoot the ball into the side pockets; vary the angle, speed, distance and use "follow", "stop" and "draw" action

Exercise 2: Passing the cue-ball back and forth between object-balls

The goal of this exercise:

- Stroke straightness
- Elbow stabilization
- Feel for ball speed
- Striking the cue-ball on its vertical axis perfectly

There is actually no better method for practicing stroke straightness, so get good at this exercise. Place the balls as described in diagram 200. In the beginning, the object balls should build an alley of "four ball widths" apart. Shoot the cue ball from the head spot into the foot rail. Strike the cue ball exactly in the middle using a soft speed to start with (1) and in-

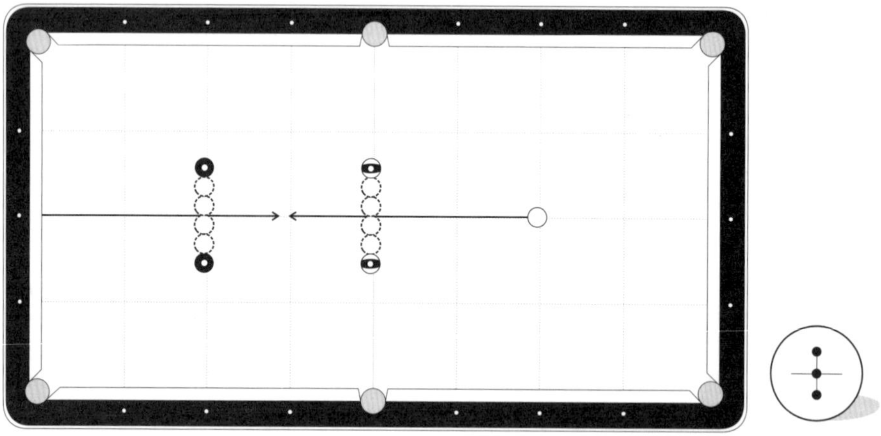

Diagram 200

crease this up to (3) or 30% of your break speed. The intention here is to drive the cue ball back and forth between the object balls without touching them. Just as in our previous exercise, technique is also imperative here as well. Attention should first be given to your cue-tip (straightness in delivery) and thereafter to the cue ball. Should the cue ball rebound into an object ball, you can understand how to correct this faster.

Training

Exercise intensification:

- Narrow the alley of balls to 3 ball widths and thereafter to 2.
- Strike the cue ball with follow and draw.
- Increase the stroke energy to 5.

Exercise 3: The stop shot using constant stroke energy

The goal of this exercise:

- Be able to produce a stop shot from various distances, using constant stroke energy.
- Stroke straightness.
- Feel development.

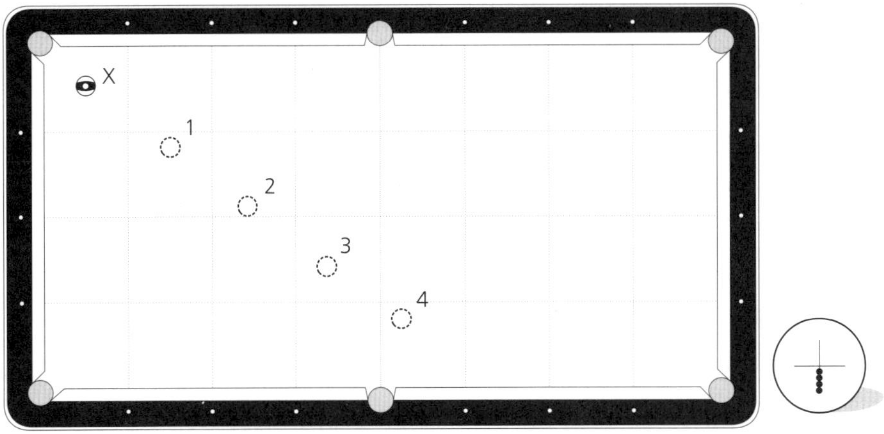

Diagram 201

Arrange the balls as in diagram 201.

This exercise requires you to practice stop shot shots from various distances (1 through 4), using a constant stroke energy. For instance, use a stroke speed of 3. Always place the object ball at "X" after each attempt, but vary the distance the cue ball has to travel from the starting points 1 through 4. Mark each of these starting points by moistening your finger or use a piece of chalk. Problems can be recognized quicker and corrected easier when the starting positions are constant. Be reminded that your mind stores the results of missed as well as made shots equally. Only through training is one able to outweigh the failure quotient through successful interactions.

Develop a feeling for a stroking speed and impress this well in your mind. Further, you must also witness the exact striking point that is required for the shot. Only through this observance afterwards is a correction possible and effective.

At the onset, one may have problems in finding the correct striking point, which may cause the cue ball to follow or draw back unintentionally. This is normal. Keep in mind that your goal here is in finding whether the striking point should be raised or lowered, so keep your stroke speed always at a constant level. Satisfy this stop shot requirement, 3 out of 5 times for each. This exercise is a great way to check stroke straightness and thereby develop and/or refine your technique.

We claim: When the player strikes the cue ball exactly on its vertical axis and this meets the object ball full and exactly in its center. The cue ball will either stop, follow or draw exactly on the line of aim.

Any waiver to the left or right (be it through cue ball English or sight picture on the object ball or both) will fall back on faulty aiming and follow through technique and a good indicator (if witnessed) how your stroke straightness needs to be corrected.

Exercise intensification:

- Greaten the distance to the object ball (4) along the long rail.
- Greaten the distance the object ball has to travel to the pocket.
- Make all of these examples 8 out of 10 times. (Cultivate, don't change your basic playing system)

Exercise 4: Stop shot using a constant striking point

The goal of this exercise:

- Technique option development

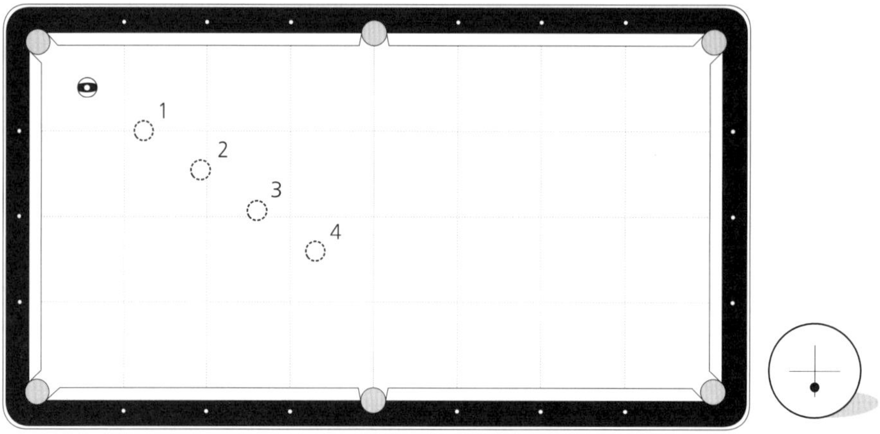

Diagram 202

- Straightness is stroke
- Elbow stabilization
- Feel development

This is of course similar to exercise 3, only now the stroke energy is a variable, and the striking point on the cue ball remains constant. Pick out a striking point between shortly under the horizontal and directly on the vertical axis to far under on the cue ball.

Exercise intensification:

The same examples as in exercise 3 apply, only here you are practicing new striking points on the cue ball as well.

Exercise 5a: The draw shot

The goal of this exercise:

- Controlled draw action development.
- Straightness in stroke.
- Elbow stabilization.
- Feel development.

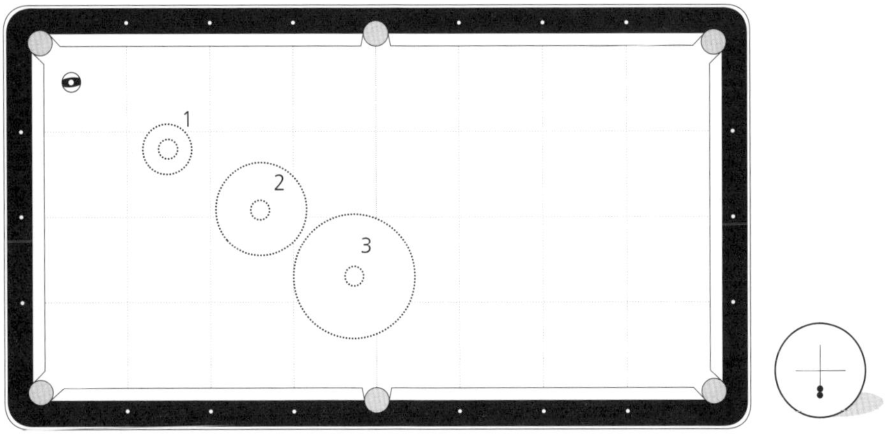

Diagram 203

The objective here is to generate enough draw action to the cue ball that it returns on or around its original starting point. The striking point on the cue ball should be aimed low in the beginning of this exercise (watch out for the "slip zone"). In doing so, especially on the first practical example, it doesn't matter greatly that the cue-ball draws back perfectly straight. You do not want to draw into the cue-tip. Therefore, offset these two balls slightly.

Marking the target area: Example 1 should be "three ball widths" in diameter, example 2 should be "five", example 3; "seven" and so on. Of five attempts, at the very least, three should be accomplished. In diagram 204, we demonstrate the measuring and marking of the target area for example 2.

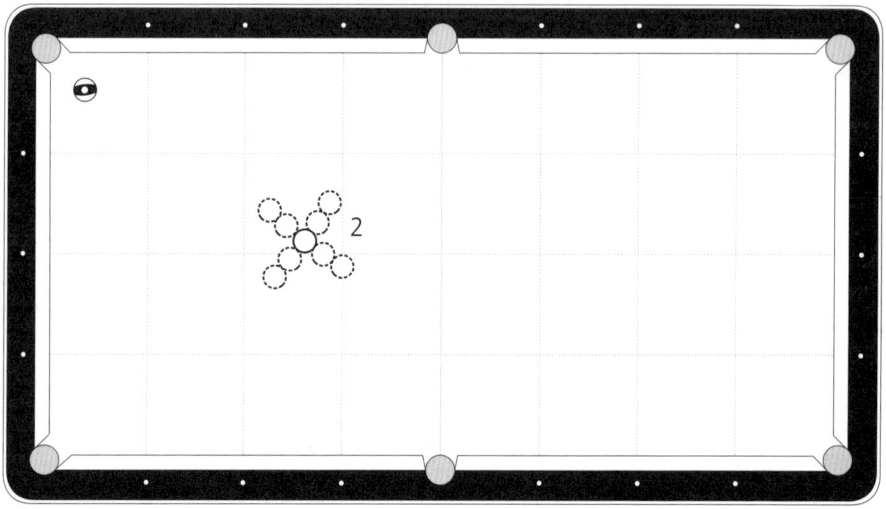

Diagram 204

Exercise intensification:

- Move the exercise further away from the pocket.
- Consciously and by design – vary the striking point on the cue ball.

Observe diagram 205; The objective here lays in drawing the cue-ball from each of the 5 "positions" back to within "two ball diameters" of position one.

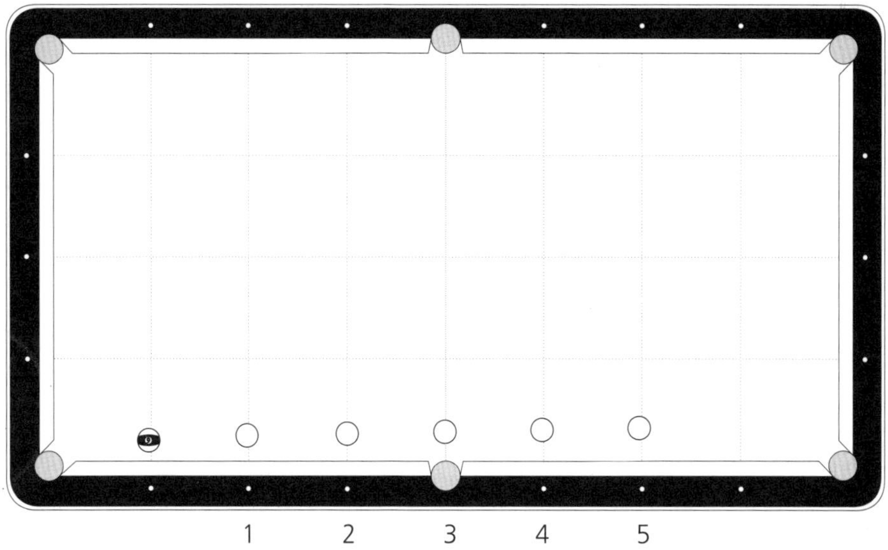

Diagram 205

Exercise 5b: The draw shot

The following exercises should only be attempted after the previous exercises are successfully accomplished 3 out of 5 times first. This exercise is related primarily to diagram 205.

Exercise intensification:

- Draw the cue ball from each of the 5 positions back to position 2.
- Draw the cue ball from each of the 5 positions back to position 3.
- Using the starting position 1 through 3, draw the cue ball back into the "foul zone".
- Using the starting position 1 through 3, draw the cue ball back into the "head rail".

Exercise 6: The follow shot

The goal of this exercise:

- Controlled follow action development.
- Straightness in stroke.
- Elbow stabilization.
- Feel development.

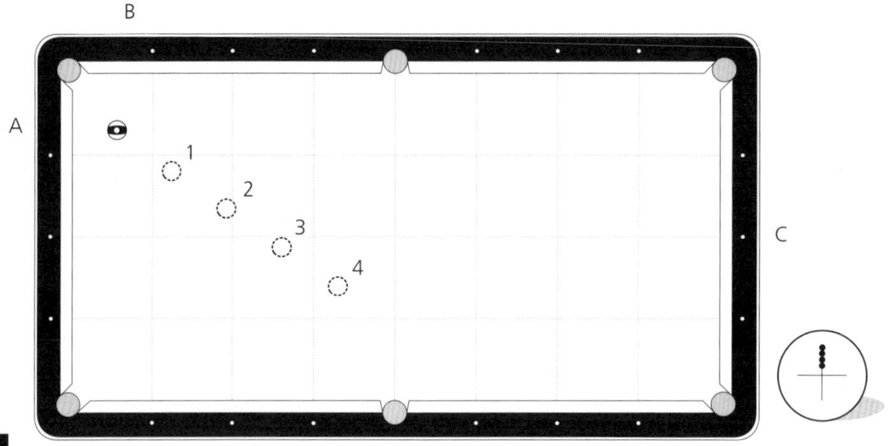

Diagram 206

The objective here is to make the "slightly offset" shot into the corner pocket and follow with the cue ball to the rail (A) and come to rest within a two ball diameter of the rail. Practice this from all four positions and achieve this goal 3 out of 5 times.

Exercise intensification:

- Raise the stroke energy enough, so that the cue ball is driven to the second rail (B).
- Raise the stroke energy enough, so that the cue ball is driven to the third rail (C).
- Move the object ball to position 1 and repeat this exercise.

6. Beginner mistakes

In this chapter, we want to touch on common mistakes which are often observed in beginners but which are sometimes apparent in an advanced player as well. Recognizing and avoiding these mistakes can positively influence ones game, mentally as well as physically. These mistakes appear mostly in ones technique. However, the mental aspect in respect to the lack of specific knowledge can also be blamed. Whereas, the one can be caused by the other and visa versa. During the growth of a player, either these mistakes disappear quickly or only after a long ordeal the player, plays around them. Whereby early awareness, is an advantage that could help one avoid these mistakes altogether. There are those however, in spite of their awareness and knowledge, who want to do it their way. It is also common, that players (over a period of several years) will imbed such failures/mistakes in their technique so deep, that it takes either a huge effort to be rid of them or they are doomed to live with them (attitude).

6.1 Faulty technique

By faulty technique, we are referring to everything that has to do with; "stance", "grip", "aiming" and "follow-through" techniques. Whereby, one cannot show a clear separation involving these four areas. For example: The best stance is nothing, when the follow-through stroke is shaky or a good stroke can let you down, at one time or another, if your closed bridge is too loose.

If one were to concentrate on removing any fault in their technique, then they are going back to the basics. Training on basic skills is of course elementary, but this builds up a player's resolve. Which is fundamentally important in supporting a positive attitude toward all situations, in any sport. The following statement should be clear to all who compete and are seriously interested in their own improvement:

Everything that does not help me advance steadily are faults that stop or slow my growth. All of which, must be "sorted out", avoided and/or worked against as soon as I am aware of them.

This is a rule, used for advancement in any sport one can think of. Of course, anyone who has ever reached a high level of play has made mistakes along the way, sometimes big ones. No getting around this and for that matter, there is no need, because mistakes are useful reminders that can help you do things right the next time. However, faulty technique is hard to see in oneself and unless they are pointed out to you, (with a great deal of tact or a marginal percent of authority) they tend to be learned very slowly if at all. Faulty technique makes progress sluggish and pushes the "date of betterment" to another period ***in the future.*** Faulty technique can be observed often, even in experienced players. However, experienced players as a rule have learned to live with them to the point where they seldom interfere with their game. Out of 500 pool players, there are two of them, who use nothing close to the basic playing system we have described here in this book. The rest of those 498 players show a good playing system, which resembles more or less the same guidelines we have presented here.

The question to you remains; whether you think it would be better to join the rest of the 498 or belong to those other two.

A tip that is always good: If at all possible, study the movements of a professional player. Observe their playing system; be aware how they separate their warm-up and follow-through stroke when aiming. Watch for those traits in their technique that always seems to be present when they play. Traits that stabilize a good, reproducible playing system. However, before deciding on copying particular traits that you have actively observed, be certain you understand the reason why it would help your own playing system.

Beginner mistakes

Another tip: Take the trouble to play the roll of the silent observer in a billiard room somewhere and observe all the players actively playing. Amateurs down to beginners will show themselves easily and can be often recognized using (much more than) one of the following characteristics:

- The player stands much more upright when aiming (head up, looking down nose).
- Just before or during the shot, the player "jumps up" abruptly.
- During the warm-up stroke, the elbow is moving up and down.
- The player uses more judgment when aiming a difficult shot, than a

controlled concerted and calculated view (chin-log).

- The cue ball is not struck by the cue-tip at that point, where originally intended (Circle of Error).
- The butt of the cue is held too tightly.
- The closed bridge holds the shaft much too loosely.
- The player does not lead his cue-stick in a straight manner and bodily movements are apparent with each stroke.
- The player does not separate the warm-up and follow-through stroke at all (suddenly explodes).
- After the shot is executed, the beginner will show body English more readily when missing a shot becomes reality.
- The cue-tip travels characteristically through the cue ball to the "left" or the "right" or is raised after contact – instead of holding a straight line to and through the cue ball.
- The player does not understand the technique behind "roughly 10 cm past". A beginner tends to stop abruptly after contacting the cue ball or when attempting a draw shot, pulls the cue back in an effort to acquire a better affect in cue-ball action.
- The butt of the cue is generally held much higher, especially for draw or stop shots and always when shooting the cue ball from the rail.
- The Novice varies his technique strongly and does not seem to have characteristic similarities to his technique. For example: They use long and short bridges illogically. Have a rushed stroke in one case and a slow stroke in another relatively similar situation. Takes time with a relatively easy situation but rush an exceedingly difficult one.
- Beginners often attempt difficult shots first and leave easier balls so they block the path for their opponents' balls. When all their balls are in place, they hope to pride themselves on a run-out. (Typical Novice 8-ball strategy) In straight pool or 14.1, they always shoot the obvious break ball early. In 9-ball they always attempt 9-ball combinations whenever they are noticed, illogical and risky.

Our next volume will give one a greater insight to better position play and shows how to turn a seemingly difficult situation into a relatively easy win. This was a list of most common errors made by amateur pool players, which, along the guidelines we have presented in this volume and to which is presented in our next volume, which should be recognized or at least worked against and overcomed with the correct practice techniques.

If we were to grade each of these faults with a "percent rate" for failure, the beginner would see a marked improvement in percentage to his game, after effectively excluding them from his playing system.

For example: When there is no separation between the warm-up and follow-through stroke, to ask the question; "Will I make this or not?". 15% of the shot result is programmed for failure. When the player does not strike the cue ball at that striking point where he originally intended to, then 25% of that shot is programmed for failure. Because the elbow is not stabilized, then 5% of that shot is programmed for failure and so on.

The sum of these impurities one finds in their own playing system, provides a rough idea on how much room for improvement one has. Therefore, we find:

The more of these errors that you can correct, the better player you will be.

Beginner mistakes

Before you can train effectively, you must of course, know first what it is you are doing wrong. Training with an experienced trainer is undoubtedly the best way to recognize them. Sound literary advice will consequently accelerate this process. However, for whatever reason, this may not completely apply in your case. At this point, if interest is still a predominant factor, then you must be honest with yourself. Be receptive to qualified advice and disciplined enough to follow a self-designed workout, which includes discovered technical deficiencies and consequently eliminate them, one by one. Remember, technical impurities, which are present during training and have a "failure factor" of say (1) on a scale of (5), will quickly be at (3) or over 50 percent, playing under pressure (i.e. Tournament play, etc.).

6.2 Tips for the actual beginner

An important prerequisite is the ability to strike the cue ball exactly in the middle. This should be the first thing anyone learns, to include speed control. In doing so, avoid hitting the left or the right side of the vertical axis until you are certain that you can always avoid English application at will. With ever increasing security and experience, depending on your ambitions, persistence and training repetition, the time this may cost you, will range from 4 to 12 weeks and more. Once this is achieved, with a relative amount of consistency and security, start striking the ball with draw and follow exactly along the vertical axis, avoiding English here as well. Impress upon yourself, the feel required for follow, draw, and stop shots. Vary the speed and the striking point on the cue ball. Observe and control this closely. Your good judgment is decisive here, when varying the striking point and/ or speed that your playing system is not influenced greatly. The principle behind the warm-up stroke (when aiming, then the pause (?) to ask the question, then the follow-through) does not change.

Use the preceding training diagrams that we have provided. These practical exercises begin quite simple, but advance with each example. You should be able to achieve 2 out of 3 easily before advancing to the next task. Be careful that you do not exaggerate, but do not give up either. Though these practical exercises may seem at the onset, quite simple, being able to execute any of them perfectly will certainly frustrate a total beginner even if he honestly understands what is required of him. The tasks involved here require, not only acceptable results that need to be repeated, but also a solid aiming and stroking technique, which needs to be followed. So do not forget, even under simple conditions: First me – then the balls. If you find that your progress, involving these exercises, begins to slow and problems begin to become readily apparent, then go back one or two diagrams and get better at these exercises. Going back two steps and advancing one, has been found the most effective way to train in billiards. Being able to strike the cue ball on its middle axis needs to sit in you securely before the world of "English" can be learned effectively. Once you have arrived at this point, our next volume of which we teach with at the "Pool School Germany", entitled "Position play in Pool", will compliment the progress you have made here fluidly. The application of English, among other interesting aspects of this sport, will be dealt with just as thoroughly.

Notice:

7. Glossary

This glossary defines words and terminology expressed in this sport, for this volume as well as our next volume.

Angle of Incidence

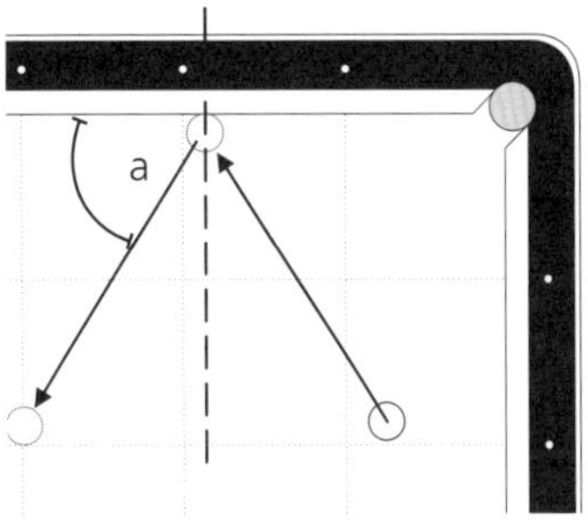

The point on the rail where the ball intends to roll into is the vertex or „intended touching point" on the rail. When building a line of reference from the vertex at right angles (90°) to the rail (X), the line of direction that the ball intends to follow can be theoretically measured against the line of reference in degrees (e) and is known as the Angle of Incidence.

(Due to innumerous application factors involved in Billiards in general, the angle of Incidence is not necessarily the Angle of Rebound.)

Angle of Rebound

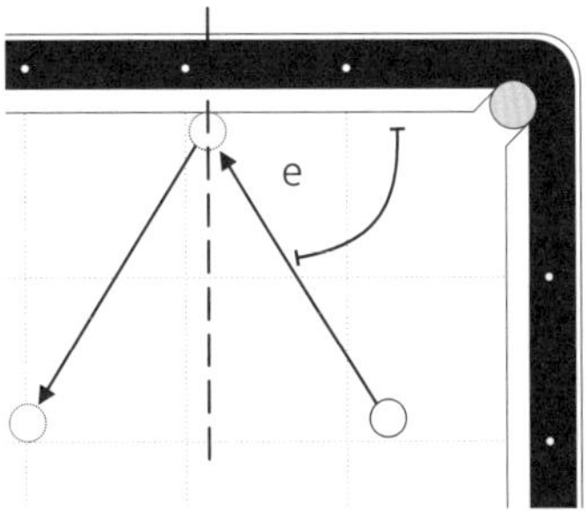

The point on the rail where the ball had struck is the vertex or „touching point" on the rail. When building a line of reference from the vertex at right angles (90°) to the rail (X), the line of direction that the ball takes after striking the vertex can be theoretically measured against the line of reference in degrees (a) and is known as the Angle of Rebound.

(Due to innumerous application factors involved in Billiards in general, the Angle of Rebound is not necessarily the Angle of Incidence.)

Glossary

Aiming line The aiming line is the line of aim leading from the center of the cue ball up to the center of the imaginary ghost ball.

Aiming point The aiming point is the center of the ghost ball (imaginary cue ball) or that point which is a half ball diameter away from the striking point on the object ball and a half ball diameter above the table surface and exactly on line with the desired direction.

Axis The Axis of a sphere (in our case „ a billiard ball") is made up of three fixed lines of reference. These lines of reference pass through the center of mass and are mutually perpendicular. The first line of reference is the principle longitudinal line in the plane of symmetry. The second line is the lateral line in the plane of symmetry and is perpendicular to the first. The third is the normal axis line and on its plane of symmetry and is perpendicular to the other two.

Striking the ball on the longitudinal line affects ball action on the vertical axis with „follow", „draw" or „stop action".

Striking the ball on the lateral line affects ball action on the horizontal axis with „left English", „right English" or „stop action".

Striking the ball on the normal axis line affects ball action on the supporting axis with „left masse´, right masse´ or cue detrimental „jump action".

Banking, banks (Bank shot) A shot to which an object ball travels against one or more rails before falling into a pocket.

Ball contact Ball contact is that point in time, where the cue tip touches the cue ball. The duration of this moment decides, for the most part, how much velocity, English or masse´ the ball is imparted with.

Ball direction The line of direction an object ball takes.

Ball in hand The allowance to place the cue ball, after an opponents foul, anywhere on the tables playing surface and start from there.

Breaking The opening stroke of a game.

Break cue A cue stick which is primarily used for the opening break, exclusively those disciplines where it is not required of the player to designate a ball off the break, i.e. 9-ball or 8-ball.

Bridge, bridge hand The bridge is so named because it bridges the gap between the guiding hand (bridge hand) and the cue ball. The bridge hand supports the striking end of the cue and is laid either on top of the hand (open bridge) or is grasped between the fingers (closed bridge). Right handed players use a left handed bridge hand.

Calling (Ball & Pocket) The required designation and identity is prematurely forecasted. For example: „8-ball... corner pocket!" How the 8-ball gets to the designated corner pocket is irrelevant as long as the cue ball remains on the playing field. While it is required in 8-ball and 14.1 to call the balls, in 9-ball „slop" is legal.

Calling (Strict) The required designation, identity and manner is prematurely forecasted. For example: 7-ball... rail first, kisses off the 2-ball and lands in the side pocket. If nothing other than this is achieved, then this is considered a legal shot. If however, the 2-ball in this example were to fall as well, then the demonstration was not forecasted correctly and the player must give the table over to his opponent.

Carom Carom is best described as useful deflection off another ball. For example: Using the surface of another object ball and making the cue ball or an object ball move in the desired direction from this surface.

Category The entire spectrum of competing participants, i.e. Ladies, Mens, Seniors, Juniors, Teams etc.

Combination (Combo) This is the expression used for making the intended object ball in conjunction with one or more object balls.

Chalk A small cube of calcium carbonate used to magnify the abrasion effect between the leather tip and surface of the cue ball. See chapter 1.4.1

Circle of Error The area struck on the cue ball face with the cue-tip that is not completely under control. Varies between (Pro) 1/20th and (Beginner) 1/3rd of an inch in diameter.

Cue ball The cue ball is the only ball allowed to be struck by the leather tip of the cue stick.

Cue tip The cue tip is made up of compressed leather and is mounted on the ferrule. Together with chalk, this is the primary portion of the cue stick that strikes the cue ball. See chapter 1.1.3

Cue stick (Cue) The only piece of playing equipment that can legally set the game of billiards in motion.

Cue axis The imaginary core line of a cue stick.

Cue span The cue span is the distance between the bridge hand and the stroking hand.

Discipline Discipline refers to the rules which apply to the individual games that are recognized by a controlling entity, i.e. B.C.A.- Billiard Congress of America or D.B.U. German Billiard Union. These entities recognize the disciplines 9-ball, 8-ball, 14.1 among others and have written rule books pertaining to the rules of these disciplines.

Drawing (the ball) (Draw shot) To draw the ball means to bring the cue ball to spin back towards you after hitting an object ball fully. It also means to strike the cue ball well underneath the horizontal axis, see chapter 4.3 The draw shot.

Diamond The embedded rail reference points (18 on pool tables and 20-24 on carom tables) to which are mostly round, however were formerly in the shape of a diamond.

End piece The end piece is that portion of the butt between the bumper and the wrap handle.

English To strike the ball anywhere left or right of the vertical axis line and impart the cue ball with side spin. Contrary to a perfectly executed „stop", „follow" or „draw ball", where absolutely no side spin is present, English is used to additionally influence deflection response – to the object ball; from the cue ball – the cue balls deflection; after rebounding off the rail as seen in angles or curves. A form of English (left or right) is blended with one of the 3 basic cue ball applications stop, follow or draw, whereby the stop line of the cue ball initiates the most „squirt". The use of „tuck" or „roll" technique removes the effects of „squirt".

Ferrule The sleeve mounted on the striking end of the cue stick shaft and situated behind the leather tip. Made up of a variety of stable materials such as hard plastic, metal or even ivory. The ferrule is the shafts last line of defence against premature damage.

Follow shot To strike the cue ball above its horizontal Axis. See chapter 4.4

Foul A foul is described in a game situation as an immediate change of player. Dependent upon actual game rules which deal with minimum requirements such as: „The cue ball must remain inside the playing field." or „The cue ball must strike an object ball and either one or the other must touch a rail afterwards." Specific rules in pool for individual disciplines vary greatly. A foul can be placed in 3 categories.

1. Normal foul
2. Tactical foul and 3. Illegal foul

The consequences involved with normal and tactical fouls are basically similar. Depending on how good your opponent is, one may or may not lose the game because of the foul.

An illegal foul will cost the player the game immediately and the following game as well.

An illegal foul can be described as any exaggerated outbreak of emotion which words or physical actions are used to intimidate and influence an opponents inner peace at the beginning or during his inning on the table. Moving a ball intentionally with the hand to obtain an advantage is also reason for illegal foul consequence.

Game point (Game) The elemental integral to a set (see set).

Ghost ball The ghost ball is the imaginary cue ball projected at the point where it should strike the object ball to drive it in a desired direction. See chapter 3.1.2.2

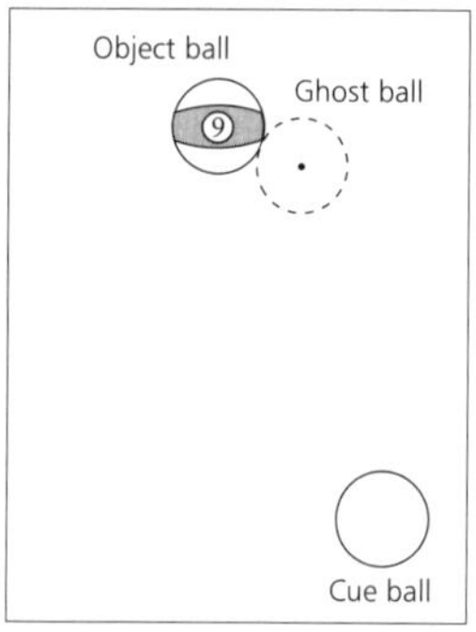

Grip See stroking hand.

Inning A players chance to perform on the pool table.

Jump shot A stroke to the cue ball designed to make the cue ball spring over an obstacle (i.e. another ball).

Kick shot To drive the cue ball into one or more rails before hitting an intended object ball. Meant to either avoid a foul, create a re-safe or both or make the object ball outright.

Glossary

Lagging Lagging is executed between opponents simultaneously upon the pool table. Both players attempt to rebound their balls off the foot rail and back to the head rail and are competing for the option to choose who will break. The opponent whose ball is closest to the head rail wins the option to choose. In 8-ball and 9-ball the break is an advantage. However, in straight pool (14.1) it is considered a disadvantage.

Match A match normally consists of one to three sets (see sets). To win a match means to defeat your opponent and advance in ranking (i.e. tournament rankings).

Massé shot When applying a masse´ shot, the cue is aimed at the cue ball from an angle anywhere above the horizontal plane and anywhere left or right of the cue balls vertical axis. Striking the cue ball with the cue stick in this manner influences the cue balls supporting axis directly. Initially the cue ball squirts away in the direction where the cue ball surface was struck with the cue tip, not aimed with the cue stick. Depending on the angle the cue stick is held to the cue ball and the amount of force applied, the cue ball attempts to curve, either heavily or slightly in the direction the supporting axis is rotating. Used to maneuver around an obstical (i.e. object balls or the edges of the playing field (pocket edges)). Masse´: French; of masser, to make a Masse´ shot. Fr. Masse = Sledge hammer.

Mechanical bridge (Bridge, crutch, grandma's helper)

A stable extension, similar (in principle) to the open bridge. Used to support and guide the shaft portion of the cue for shots too far away for the normal physical reach of the player. There are two types of mechanical bridges:

1. The basic extension, where freedom of application is not obstructed.
2. The elevated extension, where freedom of application due to other balls is obstructed.

Mechanics of technique How your playing system physically begins and sets the cue ball into motion to include proper conclusion (where the cue tip comes to rest).

Miscue This is what happens when cue ball contact with the leather tip is prematurely interrupted, causing the tip to slip off the cue ball.

Object ball Any of the 15 numbered playing balls intended to be moved or pocketed through the use of the cue ball.

One railer See Banking, Bank shot (Banks)

Piqué French for pricking, however in our case it is a stroke where the cue is aimed at an angle to the cue ball above 45° to 50° to the table surface and control cue-ball movement after the hit.

Pocket tolerance The pocket tolerance is the width a pocket has that still offers an object ball to fall into it. A practical way to find this is to measure the pocket using the diameter of two balls placed next to each other in the pocket opening.

Pocket (In the jaws) (In the subway)

When the object ball bounces back and forth between the opening of the pocket, you may hear the expression „He rattled it in the jaws!" meaning: the object ball didn't go into the pocket.

When you make a shot on a table with automatic ball return (regardless which pocket an object ball falls into, they roll on a rail system in the table to a gathering box located at the foot of the table) you may hear the expression „It" (the object ball) „was sent in the subway!".

Any of these expressions deal with the pool table pockets. When playing under calling conditions (see calling) the pocket must be clearly designated, at best when pointing with the cue stick at the intended pocket and saying: „8 ball in the (corner) or (side) pocket".

Re-safe A re-safe involves completing the minimum requirements to the rules of that discipline, whereby you are clearly inhibited and turn the table over to the opponent with at least a similar outlook or more difficult. Re-safe means to solve a difficult problem (presented to you by your opponent) by creating a new problem for your opponent. Resafeing your opponent requires much insight, experience, imagination and knowledge of the rail system, see safety play.

Running out (the table) (Run out or „to run")

A run out or running the table is described as completing a game, beginning from the break up to and making the winning ball at the end. Whereby, here the opponent is given no opportunity to perform and loses that particular game.

Safety play Here a player has no good opportunity to continue his inning without risking much. The decision to play a safe at this point may be very wise. The player chooses here to complete the minimum requirements to the rules of play, but so, that his opponent also has no good opportunity to make his next objective without risking a great deal more.

Scratch When the cue ball falls unintentionally into a pocket.

Set A set states the objectives involved toward completing a match (normally one set during normal tournament qualification and double elimination, however the best of three, five or more sets may be observed between top contenders and single elimination in greater tournaments as the field narrows) between opponents (normally two players). Game points or games that need to be won to complete a set can vary from 2 to endless, but normally between 5 and 11 games. This means if two players were to compete in a race to 7, the maximum number of possible games that could be played is 13 (7:6).

Sharking Sharking the opponent can be described as a timed and tactful disturbance from the seated opponent (i.e.: pouring ice water in a water glass, whispering with a spectator, etc.) in order to redirect the playing opponents concentration away from a particular shot situation where it is gravely needed. Sharking can be tactful or tactless but is always illegal and the consequences involved if accused of sharking range from a warning to an outright loss of game.

Shot direction The shot direction is the direction to which the cue is aiming.

Slip zone The slip zone is the cue balls outer most ring and is approximately one third of an inch or one centimeter in width. See chapter 1.4.1.2

Slop As long as the initial requirements of the discipline are met, i.e. in 9-ball: (The lowest numbered ball must be struck first), where or how an object ball falls into a pocket is thereafter considered a legal shot.

Squirt or deflection When hitting the cue ball with left or english, the cue ball will slick away from the line of aim and follow the direction opposite that point on the cue ball surface where it was struck by the cue tip.

Stop shot To play a stop shot means to bring the cue ball to a complete stop after hitting the object ball fully. It also means to strike the cue ball on or just under the horizontal axis strongly (see chapter 4).

Striking point (on the cue ball)

The striking point on the cue ball means the point on the cue ball where it is struck by the leather cue tip.

Striking point (on object ball) The striking point on the object ball is that point that needs to be struck by the cue ball or another object ball that directs it in the desired direction. The striking point is on line with the desired direction and is normally a half ball diameter from the table surface, exceptions may occur during the break or when executing a jump shot.

Stun shot The stun shot is used in a situation where the cue ball needs to move either to the left or the right (90°) from the point of impact on the object ball. However the shot situation is such, that both are aligned exactly and usually close to the pocket. By using stop shot action and maximum pocket tolerance, shooting hard brings the cue ball to move in the desired direction. The use of opposite english to desired cue ball direction offers additional security and distance. Keep in mind the affect „squirt" has.

The stroking hand That hand that moves the cue stick to and through the cue ball. See chapter 2.2.2

Throwing (a ball) When two object balls are pressed against each other or have a space between them no more than an eight of an inch and are aligned for example, a ball width to the „left side" of a given pocket. Hitting the „left side" of the ball closest to you will „throw" the second ball in the combination to the right. Observing such an example that stretches the entire length of the table, greater insight to the mechanics of „throwing" can enable the player to redirect the second ball up to and over a diamond in width.

Warpage Warpage is seen as the conditions a cue has been subjected to from weather elements, i.e. cue storage in a car, on a hot summer day and during times when the humidity level is very high or frosty and very cold. Cues made of wood that are subjected to these conditions regularly will eventually lose their original manufactured straightness and begin to „bend" or „warp".

Index

T

U

V

W

Y

Epilogue

We hope that our initial volume has helped you toward the betterment of your game. However, theoretical knowledge alone has never turned a nobody into a successful pool player overnight, but rather practice, practice, practice....

If you wish to contact us to obtain more information or have more questions pertaining to the Pool School Germany, want to criticize or express a point or gratitude then write to us at:

www.poolschool.de

More Informations:
www.thepoolschool.com

What is the POOL SCHOOL GERMANY?

The Pool School Germany is the first exclusive Pool School in Germany where the curriculum and training procedures are based upon the same fundamentals applied at the Pool School USA. The Pool School USA is a renowned American Pool Billiard academy based in Madison, Wisconsin. The Pool School USA is administrated by one of the most experienced and successful Pool Billiard trainers worldwide, Mr. Jerry Briesath.

About the founders of the POOL SCHOOL GERMANY

In March 1992, David Alfieri (a German National Champion) and Uwe Sander (a European Champion) visited the Pool School USA academy, in order to qualify and achieve their BCA trainer license. During a 14 day Seminar/Training (the first of three blocks) Jerry Briesath conveyed practically all important information about Pool Billiards.

During the same year in September 1992, Jerry Briesath visited the Pool School Germany and helped them tremendously with the grand opening. Here, Jerry Briesath gave David and Uwe an additional refresher course, whereby the opportunity presented itself to video tape his teaching methods. These video tapes serve the Pool School Germany as intensive study material and teaching guidelines to which has been extremely effective.

In June 93 both David and Uwe completed the 3rd level of the BCA instructor course (advanced level). At this point in time upon completion of this course, both David and Uwe were the only official BCA instructors in Germany; in Europe there was a BCA (officially certified) instructor in Switzerland and in Sweden.

How does the POOL SCHOOL GERMANY teach?

The Pool School Germany is equipped with exclusively designed training rooms. The equipment provided is of high quality and give the student the opportunity to study and learn with „high tech" training aids along with qualified instructor guidance in a relaxed, simple but effective manner. Consequently the student learns more and achieves results faster.

Up until June 1997 well over 600 students had attended the courses at the Pool School Germany. Their reactions to the teaching methods here have proven to be positive, in that many of these students have come back for refresher courses or have attended intensive training blocks for individual problem areas.

At this point we would like to thank all of our students who have done there part in helping the Pool School Germany become so successful.

The modern methods used at the Pool School Germany to teach pool billiards has up to this point, yet to expand broadly in Germany, let alone Europe. It focuses mainly on methods that help the player save time – in the form of years – that a normal player looses when following false examples because of incomplete basic knowledge. The normal player nurtures an unstable foundation. Problems with movement preparations are adapted and become accustomed to and eventually the player learns to play around them. However, getting accustomed to these problems take years, many years.

The Pool School Germany help the player identify these individual problems which negatively influence their game and help the player to remove them completely and understandably which leads them to a stabile foundation quicker. The PSG also relates and offers basic theoretical knowledge, of course but also designs individual training programs which bring the student to master easy and eventually difficult situations regularly on a self paced basis. The main stream knowledge includes technical (aiming systems, stroking technique, etc.) as well as tactical knowledge concerning specific disciplines.

Research Material

THE SCIENCE OF POCKET BILLIARDS, from Jack H. Koehler (1989), Sportology Publications, 25832 Evergreen Road, Laguna Hills, CA 92653

A great and recommended book for those who wish to have Pool Billiards explained in a scientific manner; because here, declarations or the Authors claims are not only presented but given in such a manner that can be reproducibly proven.

BILLIARDS – THE OFFICIAL RULES & RECORDS BOOK, under the Billiard Congress of America, www.bca-pool.com

A well organized and prepared Documentation on Pool Billiards of which to learn about the sporting rules as well as interesting Historical background information, to include; playing rules for all disciplines, scoring tables, top player introductions (Hall of Fame) and new playing varieties are given here. More or less an all-round book which is revised regularly.

Notice:

Notice:

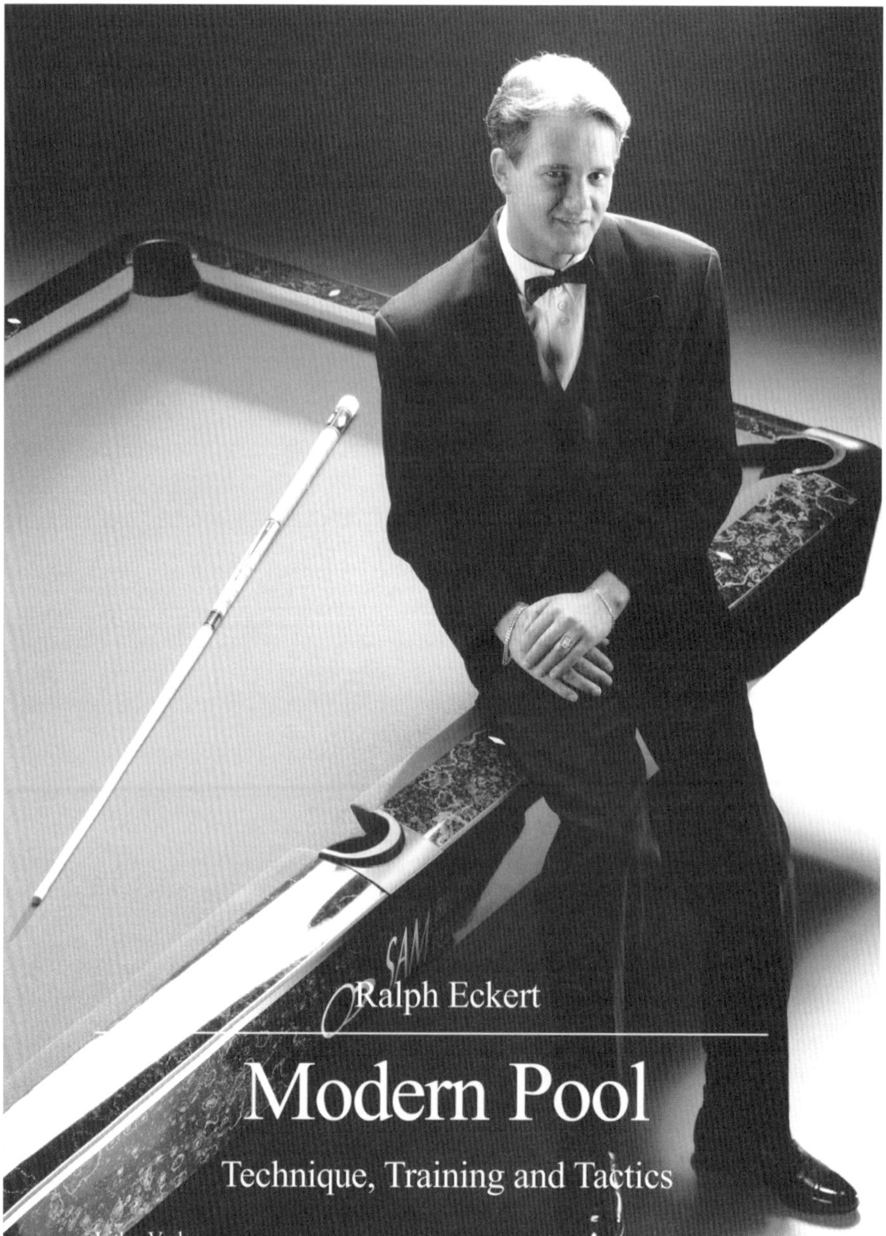

billiardbook.com

Other books from LITHO-Publishers

Modern Pool

by Ralph Eckert

Modern Pool is the German Classic among Billiard Literature in Germany. Printed in English since 1 April 2005. This book is admired for its comprehensive illumination on the subject of Pool Billiards. With this Book, Ralph Eckert has put a complete study and training program together that turns the Beginner into an Advanced player in Pool. It closes those gaps of knowledge that is important in learning the finer points of real play. He shows you how to stroke correctly, together with his training program through over 300 defined graphic illustrations that brings you to understand that Pool is much more than mastering the rules of the game. Over 40 photographs show proper playing equipment and a correct stance. This Book has great depth and is the right work for a beginner wanting to learn this sport. Advanced players can use this to learn this game from another point of view and/or discover problem zones, when they have come to that point in their game, where progress has slowed or stopped. Through the conduction and method of training as revealed by the Author, this shows one a fascinating way to help one help themselves. The Author is well known as being one of the best players in Germany and has gathered this knowledge from the past ten years of personal teachings and supplemented this with a good pound of American knowhow that he learned in the States. This was the first time an active professional pool player in Germany marketed his "Tips and Tricks" in a complete Book. Due to Eckert's knowledge and experience he has advanced to the ranks of Germans best trainers and has been awarded by the EPBF (European Pocket billiard Federation) the title Europe-Trainer.

320 Pages

Format: 17 x 24 cm • 6.7" X 9.5"

1st Copyright: 2005 (English), actual 1st Edition

Price: 45,00 USD

ISBN 3-9804706-5-2

soon available

Positioning in Pool Billiards (english)

Volume 2

ISBN: 3-9810400-3-1

and

Fundamentos del Billar Pool (espagñol)

Tomo 1

ISBN: 3-9810400-4-X

billiardbook.com